BELLS AND TALES

Stories of Amazing
Missions Moments

BELLS AND TALES

Stories of Amazing Missions Moments

ROSALIE HALL HUNT

Bells and Tales: Stories of Amazing Missions Moments

© 2024 Rosalie Hall Hunt

All Rights Reserved

Cover Design: Eric Hudiburg

Cover: Digitalized photo of Esther Lo as a six-year-old child in Fujian Province, China.

ISBN 978-1-955295-41-3

100 Manly Street
Greenville, South Carolina 29601
CourierPublishing.com

PUBLISHED IN THE UNITED STATES OF AMERICA

Endorsements for *Bells and Tales: Stories of Amazing Missions Moments*

Each time I finish reading a book by Rosalie Hunt, I think, "This is my new favorite." It's a good thing each chapter is an individual story because this is a page turner. Children will not be able to go to bed until they know the rest of the story. The narratives are compelling and engaging. Find a comfortable chair and be blessed yet again by one of the best storytellers of our generation. Great is the legacy Rosalie Hunt is leaving for future generations.

Sandy Wisdom-Martin
Executive Director-Treasurer
National Woman's Missionary Union

Who better to share stories of beloved missionaries and missions advocates than missions legend Rosalie Hall Hunt? Rosalie brings a unique vantage point with an expansive variety of family and personal connections to historical figures as well as modern-day saints. She has a foot in both worlds and serves to keep us all connected through her intriguing storytelling ability.

Jennifer David Rash
President and Editor-in-Chief
TAB Media Group

Rosalie Hunt is a master storyteller and has once again given us great stories to share with the next generation. What a life-changing opportunity for children to experience stories of missions heroes sharing God's love with the world!

Heather Keller
Missions Consultant
Girls in Action/Children in Action/Acteens
National Woman's Missionary Union

The wonderful storyteller Rosalie Hunt has done it again. This time she tells us it was her mother who taught her how to share these incredible true stories of the lives of missionaries who came before us. She tells the stories from an autobiographical perspective, which makes them that much more intriguing. Her captivating style keeps the reader engaged to the end, making you want to start the next story. Through her words, I have *met* the giants of our faith. Their lives and words impact my faith and life!

David George
President Emeritus
National Woman's Missionary Union Foundation

I love the way Rosalie brings a story to life. As she tells the stories, I am so drawn into the lives of the people.

Connie Dixon
National President
Woman's Missionary Union

I began reading books by Rosalie Hall Hunt in 2006. That first book was *Bless God and Take Courage: The Judson History and Legacy*. Since then I have read every book she has written and listened to every monologue she has presented. Rosalie is a master storyteller. Her stories appeal to our senses and our emotions — and impact us in a powerful way. So make a cup of tea or a cup of coffee and sit in your favorite chair to enjoy these stories. Rosalie knows how to tell a story *right*.

Ruby Fulbright
Executive Director Emeritus
WMU North Carolina
Vice President Emeritus
North American Baptist Women

With each word, Rosalie Hunt invites her reader to fully immerse themselves in the lives of those about whom she writes. While written primarily for young readers, *Bells and Tales* will certainly appeal to the "less than young" as well and ignite in them a desire to learn more about these missions heroes and claim them for their own.

Peggy Darby
President
Woman's Missionary Union Foundation
(First woman to hold this position)

Rosalie Hunt has done it again. What a blessing to "sit at her feet" and listen as she recounts God's faithfulness through His mission servants. I found myself anxious to read to the end and was left inspired to lead on in the days ahead.

Candace McIntosh
Executive Director
Alabama Woman's Missionary Union

Dedication

To: Esther Lo Ping Ren Wu, my treasured friend and prayer partner from college days at Oklahoma Baptist University

And: Alice Newman, remarkable leader of WMU women of Hawaii, and beloved of all privileged to know her

Table of Contents

Foreword		xiii
Preface		xv
Acknowledgments		xvii
Chapter 1	Esther and the Giant Bell	1
Chapter 2	The Old Man on the Steps	11
Chapter 3	Ann and the Silk Umbrella	19
Chapter 4	Adoniram and the Priceless Pillow	31
Chapter 5	Hephzibah Jenkins Townsend Tells Her Own Story	45
Chapter 6	Annie at Home on the Range	57
Chapter 7	Fannie Finds a Way	71
Chapter 8	Kathleen Mallory: The Tiny Dynamo	85
Chapter 9	Gladys Aylward: Small Woman, Giant Heart	97
Author's Note		113
Bibliography		115

Foreword

The phrase "saved by the bell" will take on new meaning as you read this compilation of short stories written by Rosalie Hall Hunt to illustrate and record the miraculous power of God working through ordinary people.

In these pages, you will read about Esther Lo Ping Ren, who was literally saved by a bell. You'll meet Hephzibah Jenkins, who was smuggled out of war-torn Charleston, South Carolina, as a newborn baby. You will encounter the spirit of Christ in the gnarled hand of a leper. You will feel the agonizing suffering of Adoniram Judson in a Burmese prison, sustained by the resourcefulness and courage of his wife, Ann. You will read about the horseback-riding Annie Armstrong and the founding of Woman's Missionary Union. Then you will marvel at the remarkable Gladys Aylward. She illustrates once again how God takes the discounted things of the world and does His mighty work. Read *Bells and Tales*: You'll be inspired, motivated, and blessed!

Dr. Gordon Fort
Senior Ambassador to the President
International Mission Board
Southern Baptist Convention

Preface

I love stories. I especially love stories about faraway places with strange sounding names. And *true* stories, about missionaries famous or just ordinary, are my favorites!

This collection of missions stories comes from among my best-loved. We didn't have a radio when I was growing up as a missionary kid (MK) in China. Television hadn't even been invented, say nothing of the internet and smartphones. My brother and I thrived on books and stories, and our favorite storyteller was Mama. She knew how to tell thrilling tales. Several of the stories in this volume I first heard at her knee.

The first story is about my dearest college friend, Esther (Lo Ping Ren), who grew up in China as had I. And, just like me, she had heard of Lottie Moon since she first learned to talk. In fact, her own grandmother had been led to Christ by Lottie Moon herself! Esther experienced an amazing encounter as a little girl. The next story is my own, telling how God placed His call on my life. It was such an individual kind of experience — exactly how God speaks in a unique way to each of us.

Other stories in this book are from the lives of some of our famous early missionaries and pioneer missions leaders. There may be some you have never heard before. It also recounts the story of an amazing missionary to China from this past century. Our family was honored to know her and call her "friend." Gladys Aylward grew up as a very ordinary and commonplace girl, and God did some extraordinary things in her and through her. They were things that changed the lives of hundreds of people and brought them to faith in Christ.

Who knows? Maybe that is what God will be doing in *your* life. It could be He already is!

Acknowledgments

True stories of true heroes inspire all of us. Mama loved to tell me stories of missionary heroes. Those heroes became very real to me. In turn, I wanted to pass those stories on. She also told me fascinating true-life tales of ordinary believers. They influenced me as well.

The family of Esther Wu has provided pictures and stories of their beloved mother, as has her husband, Dr. Sammy Wu. Cindy Goodwin, archivist at national Woman's Missionary Union, and Kyndal Owens, archivist for International Mission Board, are consistent sources of information both current and historic. Their love for history is obvious. Children's consultant for national WMU, Heather Keller, is the resident expert for all matters related to youth and how they learn about missions. Her insight is a blessing.

Bells and Tales: Stories of Amazing Missions Moments is very much a family project. Grandson Eric Hudiburg designed the cover and edited all the pictures. Alice Hunt, our daughter, handled both final editing, layout, and production. Ella Robinson, who has assisted me as copy editor for the last nine books, seems like part of the family by this time. We are so blessed.

BELLS AND TALES

Stories of Amazing Missions Moments

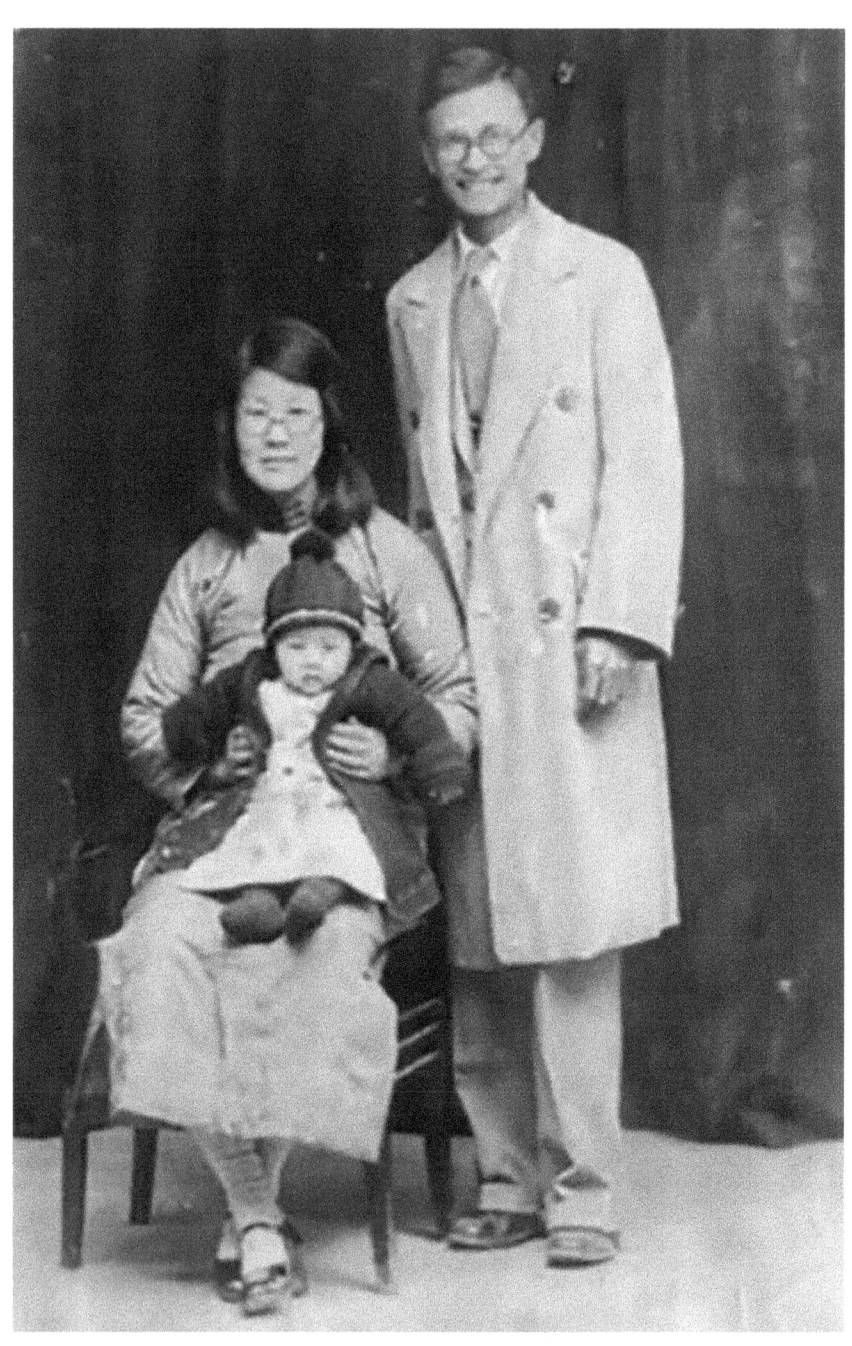

Esther as a baby — with her parents in southwest China.

Chapter One

Esther and the Giant Bell

Boom! Hisssss! The piercing, screaming, noise hit Esther's ears like a looming menace from the far side of China's purple mountains. She and her three Sunday school friends were happily headed home after Bible class when their world changed in an instant. Six-year-old Esther stopped suddenly, her bright brown eyes widening in fright as she grabbed her friend Penny's arm. With her mouth gone suddenly dry with fear, Esther gasped, "It's Japanese planes coming — we have to run!"

Every day, Mama cautioned her, "Esther, the minute you hear that hissing sound — even if it sounds far away — you must run to safety. Wherever you are, head for cover. The Japanese bombers are fast — and deadly." Mama Su Wen always shook her head to emphasize the danger. "Find a safe place."

Esther and Penny and their two pals stood staring at each other in terror. Feeling the bitter taste of fear in her mouth, Esther pointed to a large structure not far away and exclaimed, "Let's run to that building. It looks strong." Even as they all four raced toward the building, Penny cast doubtful eyes at the structure and exclaimed, "But, Esther, that's a heathen temple. We *never* go there." Gasping for air, Esther called over her shoulder, "But there is no other safe spot. Hurry! Hurry!" She had to shout over the roar of air raid sirens that suddenly pierced the air as if screaming: *Find shelter ... find shelter ... find shelter.*

The noise of the approaching bombers grew so loud that it drowned out the blaring of the sirens. As the bombers drew closer and closer, the children could hear the dreaded hissing sound as one bomb after another hit the ground. Each boom was closer than the one before. Fear forced the children's small feet to move faster and faster. Finally, they breathlessly reached the foyer of the temple, with its huge iron bell hanging from the high ceiling. Just beyond them was the main entrance of the massive Buddhist temple, and the heavy scent of burning incense wafted out to the foyer where four frightened children stood, panting for air.

Fear lent urgency to Esther's voice as she called out to the worshippers standing by the altar. "Please, please, can we come in for shelter? The bombers are coming. We are scared. Please! Oh, please!" she begged. An elderly man peered intently at the little girl, then quickly shook his head, "No! No! No!" he responded emphatically. "You children are Christian. You will bring us bad luck. Go!" he commanded with a dismissive wave of his arms. In desperation, Esther pleaded yet again, "Oh, sir, may we at *least* stay out here in the bell tower? We won't come in. I promise." Inside the building, the worshippers looked at one another and frowned. They heard the old man speak to the girls, "As you please, but do *not* come inside."

Even though her eyes were wide with fear and dread, echoing in Esther's mind was Mama's daily reminder: "Esther, we may be at war, but wherever you are, God is with you. He will protect you. Never forget — *never forget.*" Taking a deep breath and going to stand in the middle of the temple foyer, she motioned to her three friends, yelling over the noise of the bombers, "Come here by me, and all of us can be together. God will be with us. He promised." Four terrified children, their arms entwined, huddled together as the sounds of the approaching planes grew to a deafening roar. Mixed with the roar was the dreaded screaming, hissing sound of bombs as they plunged through the thick air and exploded with a deafening crash upon hitting the ground.

Suddenly, there was a huge thud — louder than all the others. In that split second, the sound of the planes strangely became a distant echo. Four huddled children all gasped in fright. And just as suddenly, they could see nothing. They stood in total darkness. That was almost as frightening as the sound of the falling bombs had been. What could possibly have happened?

In those moments so filled with uncertainty and terror, there flashed through Esther's young mind the Bible stories she had heard all her life. She recalled Mama telling her about God and His Son, Jesus, how Jesus had come to earth so He could save us from our sins and give us eternal life. In that very instant, so filled with dread and uncertainty, Esther knew she could trust Jesus. She invited Him to come into her heart and give her everlasting life. Amazingly, even in the middle of the most frightening experience of her young life, Esther felt a remarkable peace. It seemed as if this peace came straight from the heart of God to her own heart.

Simultaneously came the thought: *Well, now I know Jesus in my heart. But here I am in absolute darkness. What now?* About this time, the children heard a nearby sound, although it seemed to reverberate from a great distance. *Boom! Crash!* Then total silence. The sound of airplanes seemed far away. The four children slowly realized the Japanese bombers were fading into the distance. No more planes. No more air raid warnings. No sound of any kind.

Four anxious, troubled children tried to take a cautious step into the inky darkness that enveloped them. Small hands reached out and, one after another, encountered something hard. Hard and unyielding. *What was going on?* Suddenly, it dawned on Esther's bright young mind: the temple bell. The giant bell had fallen on them. God had provided an iron bomb shelter for His little children. "Just think!" Esther's voice sounded suddenly excited. "It's the bell! God made a bomb shelter for us with a giant bell!" All the children exhaled with sudden relief, and Penny spoke up, "But the bell! The bell is so heavy! We can't lift it off!" Four sets of anxious little hands began to dig up enough dirt to make a hole so they could get out from under the huge bell. What had been their God-sent bomb shelter had turned into a prison with no escape.

Four brave young sets of hands dug and dug until their energy was gone and their hands were scratched and bleeding. Their little hole finally became large enough to let in some air, but far too small to provide a way of escape. Esther heard a little sniff, and then another one, as if someone was trying not to cry. She bravely called out, "Let's sing — we all love to sing." Four young voices sang China's favorite hymn, "*Yesu Ai Woe*" (Jesus Loves Me).

"Let's yell!" one of Esther's pals suggested. "Let's all yell together and see if someone hears." It felt like hours as they yelled and screamed until their small throats hurt and their voices grew hoarse. After what seemed like forever, the youngsters heard a voice that sounded far in the distance calling out, "Hello. Hello. Is there someone under this bell? We hear noises." All four children began screaming anew, "Yes! Yes! Please help us get out. The bell is too heavy!"

"*Deng yi sha, Deng yi sha,*" the voices called out in Chinese. "Just wait a minute. We will get some help. This bell is huge." And as the children waited, all sorts of thoughts raced through their young minds. Esther sat in the darkness, thanking God for saving her. She got a little smile on her face as she thought, *God has saved me and given me eternal life, and now He has saved us from the Japanese bombs.* Esther thought about how much she loved her mama and her family, and how she thanked God for sparing her life.

Esther's family story was a bit sad, because when she had been only eleven months old, her birth mother, Lo Shui Tsen, died of typhoid fever. But God gave her Aunty Lo Su Wen, who became like her real mother. Aunty's brother, Lo Han, was Esther's father. He moved to Indonesia to be principal of a Chinese high school. Lo Han planned to settle there and come back to get his sister, Aunty Su Wen, and his baby daughter, Esther. But then, war with Japan started and there was no way for him to get back into China. War was a terrible thing. Esther hated it. She hated the hurt and death it brought to so many people. But even during the thoughts tumbling around in her mind, Esther was recalled to the present. She and her friends were in real danger right now.

God had miraculously saved them with a bomb shelter, but now they were trapped! All four kept reassuring each other that help would come. Those voices had promised to come back. However, each minute seemed like half an hour, and four young stomachs began to growl with hunger. They had no food or water in many hours. But the most important thing had to be rescue.

"Hello! Hello! Are you in there?" Sure enough, the voices were back, and the relieved children yelled in chorus, "Yes! Yes! Yes! Please help." The next twenty minutes felt like an entire day to four weary young children. All of them stared intently as a sliver of light began to shine in at the spot where they had bravely dug. Next a metal bar came ever so slowly into view. Before their wondering eyes, Esther and her buddies watched as the metal pole served as a crowbar. With the efforts of a group of strong men, the massive bell was finally lifted off the children, and the bright light of the late afternoon sun shone into their startled eyes.

The villagers who had gathered to watch rejoiced with great

excitement as they stared into the faces of four dazed young children, safe and sound after hours in a God-sent bomb shelter. Esther, Penny, and their friends looked around in utter disbelief, scarcely able to believe their eyes. Just yards from where they stood were the ruins of the Buddhist temple. Nothing was left standing. The temple had been totally destroyed. Not one of the worshippers had survived. Esther and her friends stood gaping at all the ruin, then turned wondering eyes to each other, realizing with chilling certainty how God had saved them from the same fate. They had just studied about miracles that morning at Sunday school — and now, here they were, still alive, thanks to God's miraculous bomb shelter. Four grateful children said in hushed tones, "Thank You, God." As Esther started for home, she turned around and looked back at the giant bell. It had been a shelter, and it had been a prison. It had been God's gift. She fervently whispered again, "Oh, thank You, God! Thank You, God!"

The Rest of the Story

After her miraculous escape from death, Esther Lo Ping Wu went on to accomplish great things for God. Her mother, Shui Tsen, had been born in Shandung Province. In fact, her mother was led to Christ by Lottie Moon herself. Shui Tsen came to faith as a young girl.

At the time of Esther's birth, her father, Lo Han, gave her an unusual name. China was an ancient land where men were always considered more important than women. But that was not the way Lo Han thought. He named their baby daughter Lo Ping Ren. *Ping Ren* means "equal responsibility." Lo Han felt a girl was just as important as a boy and had equal responsibility and value. Esther's birth mother had been Aunty's closest friend when they were in seminary together. Esther was like her own beloved child.

Esther grew up understanding that God had a special plan for her life. After the war, she and Mama Su Wen were able to move to Indonesia, where Aunty continued her missionary work and where Esther finished high school, graduating from the 3,000-student school where her father was principal. When Esther entered the school as a freshman, she was the only Christian student in the entire school and her class nicknamed her "Hallelujah Lo." Esther took it with good humor and was a shining example of the difference Jesus makes in a life. By the time she graduated, there were *other* believers in the school, because Esther had led them to Christ. Two of these were the Yao sisters who became her dearest friends. The sisters had decided they wanted to go to college in Communist China. That made their father, a wealthy rubber plantation manager, very worried about his girls, but after Esther led them to faith in Christ, the sisters decided instead to go to college in America. In gratitude, their father also paid Esther's way through college as well. All three graduated from Oklahoma Baptist University.

Years later, Esther and Samuel Wu, a childhood pal from the early school years in China, fell in love and married. Dr. Samuel Wu studied and received three medical degrees, and Esther became a Doctor of Theology, investing her life in teaching and sharing the good news. Esther and Sammy Wu have three beautiful daughters. All three of them are spending their lives helping people and sharing the story of God's love, just as their mother has. Each of the girls knows well the story of their mother, Esther, and the Godsent bomb shelter. They love to pass on to others the tale of the miracle of the bell.

Esther as a toddler in China, in her grandmother's arms.

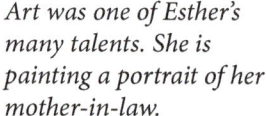

Esther as a little girl in China.

Art was one of Esther's many talents. She is painting a portrait of her mother-in-law.

Esther and Sammy Wu with daughters Rebekah, Elizabeth and Sarah.

Esther and Sammy Wu with Rosalie Hunt in Virginia, 1980s.

Beggar man in China

Chapter Two

The Old Man on the Steps

The Author's Story

His eyes. They were haunting. Hollow. Hopeless. As I stood at the porch door looking down at the beggar kneeling on the concrete steps, those hopeless eyes haunted me. My first Christmas in Zhenjiang, China, was certainly not starting off like I thought it would.

I woke early that morning — cracking one eye open and then the other. A little smile spread across my face — Christmas! Finally here. I had been feeling a bit sorry for myself because this year we couldn't spend Christmas in America with our grandparents and friends. They were ten thousand miles away. Here, in central China in 1947, there were no jolly Santa Clauses standing on every street corner with a "Ho Ho Ho." No Christmas carols playing in every store, or people passing on the sidewalk calling out "Merry Christmas!" I was nine years old and living in a big, crowded city that didn't seem to know that this was the most wonderful time of the year. Of course, there were Mama and Daddy and my older brother, Art (although he could be irritating because he thought a younger sister didn't know as much as he did). And Aunt Grace lived right next door. She was Mama's oldest sister and had been a missionary in China even longer than Mama and Daddy had. She was teaching me how to knit, and this Christmas morning I was planning to wear the bright green sweater that Aunt Grace had just finished knitting for me.

It was 1947, and Mama had worked hard to make it seem like a familiar American Christmas. Back when I was just a toddler, during the Japanese occupation of China, Daddy and Mama were forced to leave China. They couldn't take all the furniture and keepsakes that we had, so they made a secret room in our house by sealing off a door. They filled that room with all the things that we could not take with us. I was only three years old then and had no memory of the secret room. Wonder of wonders! That little room had miraculously escaped the eyes of the Japanese soldiers who occupied our house during World War II. And now, behold, all the family treasures my parents had saved in the secret room were safe and sound. These little treasures included Christmas tree ornaments that were full of sentimental value. Those ornaments now adorned our tall, live Christmas tree.

Even breakfast would be special this morning, with a pile of fresh hot biscuits and strawberry jam Grandmama Wells had sent from South Carolina. It was like a taste of home. I always loved to eat, but food wasn't a top priority this cold winter morning. I wanted breakfast to get over so we could open those stuffed Christmas stockings hanging invitingly by the fireplace. Then we would tear into that pile of presents heaped under the tall, fragrant pine tree, with its bright lights and ornaments old and new. We all sat around the large dining table while Daddy first read the wonderful story of Jesus' birth for our morning devotion. Then it was finally breakfast time.

Biscuits with lots of butter was a special Christmas treat. Butter in China was hard to come by, and this butter came in a tin, of all things. Just as I was finishing my second buttery biscuit, we heard the *tap, tap,*

tap of a knock at the front door. All of us at the table looked at each other, a bit surprised to hear a knock. We usually knew if there was someone coming to our house. A wall surrounded our two mission houses (ours and Aunt Grace's), because robbers were very common in China back then. "I'll go see who it is," I volunteered, thinking I could make short work of this interruption right at present-opening time.

Our house had a large screened-in porch with cement steps leading up to the door. It was cold and windy that Christmas morning, and I shivered a bit in the new sweater Aunt Grace had knitted for me. To my surprise, I could not see anyone when I got to the porch door. Then, looking down, I saw the man. He was ragged and old, kneeling there on the cold concrete steps looking up at me. I gazed with wide eyes at his hands that were stretched up to me, begging. The old man's hands were gnarled and twisted; he had only stumps of fingers. Part of his nose was eaten away, as were his ears. Both feet were bare in the freezing December air, but it was his eyes that haunted me. They were so hopeless, so full of despair. In an instant I realized, *Oh, dear God, this man is a leper. His body is being eaten away by leprosy. Dear Lord, how could this poor old man have managed to climb up all the cobblestones and all these steps on his knees?*

Looking up at me, the beggar with those hopeless, desolate eyes spoke in a cracked voice, "*Ching gáy wó myan baw chr bah. Woe ùh szle*" (Please give me some bread. I'm starving). My heart wrung with pity, I quickly replied, "*Dung ee shah*" (Wait a minute). Suddenly, presents and stockings were far from my mind. I hurried to the kitchen and gathered up a handful of bread and biscuits that we had had for breakfast. Returning to the cold and windy porch, I saw that the leper had not moved at all. His gnarled old hands were still lifted up, pleading for something to eat, any kind of food.

(This happened over seventy years ago, but that moment is as clear in my mind now as if it happened this morning.) I took the biscuits and bread and carefully placed them in his outstretched hands. The beggar was shaking so badly in the cold winter air that two of the biscuits dropped on the dirty steps. He looked intently at me, then looked down at the two crumbled biscuits scattered on the concrete. First putting the bread and the rest of the biscuits in his pockets, the leper next took those stumps of fingers, and with shaking fingers carefully picked up every single crumb. He kept repeating, "*Wö buh néng dzàu tah, wö uh sźle*" (I can't waste any, I'm starving).

That moment is now frozen in time in my memories. I stood there weeping, a nine-year-old child. God distinctly spoke to my heart in that instant. Without hesitation, I responded to that call: *Lord, someday let me come back to China and tell people like this that YOU are the Bread of Life.*

My heart felt like it was bleeding as I watched the leper finish eating the biscuit in his shaking hands, then slowly, haltingly make his way back down those steps, over the rough cobblestones, and down to the gate. Through eyes blurred by tears, I watched him make his painstaking way out the entrance. It dawned on me: *I don't even know his name. But he has surely changed my life.* Quickly following on that thought was the verse in Matthew 25:40 where Jesus told His disciples, "Inasmuch as you have done it unto the least of these my brethren, you have done it unto me." I cried once more. *Oh God, I just wish I could have done more.*

I went back to the dining room where the family patiently waited for me, wondering what could be taking so long. I was still a young child far from America and family and all that was familiar. However, I was not the same. I had had a Christmas guest that morning that had changed the direction of my life. The sacred vow I had just made was forever imprinted indelibly on my heart.

Thank God, He did just that. I would see many more despairing eyes and hungry hearts like those of the beggar. I would hear more cries for help and have opportunities to fulfill the vow made that Christmas morning so long ago. Thank God He sent that beggar to our door. He changed my life.

The Rest of the Story

I would see many more eyes like those of the leper. I would hear many more cries for help. Some were audible. Some were seen in the eyes of suffering, needy, despairing people in several different countries. I have had many opportunities to fulfill the vow I made that Christmas morning seven decades ago.

Sure enough, I grew up and married Bob Hunt. Long before we ever met, God had also spoken to his heart about going as a missionary to China. We were able to spend our careers telling Chinese people like that beggar that Jesus is indeed the Bread of Life. Some of those needy people were beggars; others were wealthy. Most of them were just regular people like we were, each with the same heart need to personally know Jesus, the Bread of Life. And all along the way, I have read the life experiences of so many missions heroes and learned *their* stories of sharing the Bread of Life.

Personally being able to *meet* some live missionary heroes has been my happy place, and I love to share their stories too. It is particularly exciting to learn about the very earliest missionaries and the brave people who made it possible for them to share God's love with people everywhere. I have also discovered that *all* of us who believe in Jesus are called by Him. The way we respond, however, is up to us. Every day I thank God for the Christmas morning visitor in China so many years ago. That leper changed my life.

Zhenjiang, China: Bob and Rosalie on steps, 1984

Zhenjiang, China: Author with grandsons Carl and Eric on steps, 2004

1811 Miniature of Ann Judson

Chapter Three

Ann and the Silk Umbrella

That steamy June night in Ava, Burma's capital city, was both hot and sticky. Typical monsoon weather was always wet and miserable. The moonless sky made the air so thick you could not see your own hand in front of you. Darkness had invaded Ann Judson's own heart three hours earlier.

She and Adoniram had been seated at the table for their simple evening meal when a booming voice called out, *"Min Gèe Amàk!"* Ann's eyes flew to Adoniram's as the words "the King calls" rang in their ears. It was what they most dreaded. The head guard of the death prison had come to arrest Ann's husband, calling him a foreign spy. Burma was at war with England, and all foreigners were considered enemies of the government.

Now, as she lay on her bed weeping, Ann kept reliving the earlier scene as the jailers threw her beloved Adoniram to the floor and bound a cord tightly above his elbows. Pull a cord too tightly, Ann knew, and permanent damage would be done to her husband's body. Adoniram Judson was dragged away to the prison as Ann stood paralyzed with dread. Mary and Abigail, the two little Burmese girls she had been teaching and caring for, screamed with fright. The Judsons' cook,

Koochil, and their dear friend and helper, *Maung Ing* (Mohng Eeng*)*, were both frozen in fear. Such a gentle man, *Ing* (Eeng) was one of the very first Christians in Burma. He stood shaking in terror as he looked at Ann and in a trembling voice asked, "What must we do now?"

Ann swallowed her panic and calmly and quietly gave each a task so their minds would stay busy. Finally getting the household settled down, Ann went to her bedroom and fell to her knees, sobbing out her fears to the Lord. So terrified was she that for the longest time, the only prayer her lips could form was, "*Oh God, oh God, oh God. What to do? What to do?*"

Hours later and exhausted from weeping, Ann's mind again went flying back to the past. Who would ever have thought things would come to such a crisis as this? America had never seemed so distant. The two Judsons were a world away from all that was known and familiar and peaceful. Now Ann's beloved Adoniram was thrown into the death prison, and she alone was responsible for her two little students, their cook, and their new convert friend, *Maung* (Mohng Eeng.) Ann felt completely helpless. Only one source of hope came to her frightened heart: God. Ann wept anew, crying out silently, "*Oh God, oh God, please help me. Give me wisdom. What must I do? I trust You. I trust You. I trust You.*"

Ann thought of Mama and Father and all her sisters and brothers, living in America. Here she and Adoniram were, far away in Burma, with heat burning down on them every day. Home was beautiful, cool little Bradford, Massachusetts, with its clean countryside and four seasons every year. Bradford wore a lovely white garment of snow every winter. It sparkled with beautiful flowers in spring and summer. Every autumn, leaves on the luscious trees turned beautiful colors of red, orange, and yellow. But, here in Ava, there was no beauty and peace like that. Instead, the whole country was covered with darkness, and the people were at war, and at the mercy of a ruthless emperor.

Ann smiled sadly to herself, recalling how often Rebekah, her mother, had declared, "Ann is my dear rambling child. I never know where she will ramble next." Remembering Mother's loving voice, another tear trickled down Ann's cheek as she sadly thought, *Oh Mama, I have rambled so far this time. I have just one help. That is God. I must take courage.*

Ann continued recalling those long-ago days, remembering the school right next door to their house. John, her father, was one of the school's founders. He and Rebekah were quite unusual, because they thought daughters needed an education just as much as sons. Ann had loved studying history and geography, and especially languages. Her older brother, John, was planning to go to sea. Young Ann didn't think it a bit fair that boys could travel and have adventures and girls couldn't. She wanted to travel too.

John and Rebekah Hasseltine and their six children were well-known citizens in the town. They went to church occasionally but were not involved in activities there. Ann, with her bright black curls and shining dark eyes, was known as the "Belle of Bradford." Everyone knew she loved to ramble, and to study as well as play and have a good time.

When she became a teenager, Ann began keeping a journal. She had no idea that fifty years later, what she wrote in her personal journal would be known and studied and admired by many thousands of people. Nor could she know that one day she would become known as the "Woman of the Century" in nineteenth century America.

When Ann was sixteen, she began to think about the condition of her soul. She struggled with those worries. Ann loved to have fun; she didn't want to worry about her soul. Somehow, she couldn't help it. A series of special meetings started at their church, just down the block from their house. Every night, Ann would slip in at the back and listen, and then go home and weep and pray. By the end of that week, she quit struggling. Late one night, in the privacy of her room, Ann fell to her knees and prayed for God to forgive her sins and be her Savior. That marked a profound change in Ann Hasseltine's life. It changed her family as well. Each one of them trusted Christ and were baptized into the membership of their Congregational church.

Now Ann began thinking about God's purpose for her life. She wanted to serve Him. But what could a young woman do? A girl was supposed to keep house and be a mother. She wasn't supposed to have a "job." This was a problem for Ann. She prayed earnestly about it, recording many of her thoughts and prayers in her journal. She wanted her life to count for something beyond herself. One day Ann wrote, "I want to be used however God wishes. He has my heart in His hand."

Then one fine June morning in 1810, Ann's Bradford church became the meeting place for a series of meetings that were held for Congregational ministers from all over New England. According to the rumors, a group of young ministerial students, from down the road at Andover Seminary, were coming to the meeting to make a bold proposal. They wanted the Congregational denomination to begin a missionary-sending society. Even the thought made Ann's heart leap. God had already been impressing her heart about the millions who had never heard about God and His love. Could this be an opportunity for her to do something for the Lord?

At noon that June day, several of the young ministers were lunch guests at the Hasseltine home. Among them was Adoniram Judson, who was the spokesperson for the seminary students. Judson took one look at twenty-year-old Ann Hasseltine, and as he later told her, "I fell in love." Ann noticed the handsome young minister as well.

Adoniram never wasted time. Exactly a month later, he wrote a letter to her, proposing marriage. Fast forward, and on February 5, 1812, Ann and Adoniram were married in the same parlor of the Hasseltine home where they had first met.

The next day, Adoniram and four other young ministers were ordained to ministry. In just two months, the newlyweds set sail from Salem Harbor, still not knowing just where God wanted them to serve. On the four-and-a-half-month trip to India, Ann and Adoniram each individually re-read the New Testament in Greek. Both realized that they needed to be baptized by immersion.

Upon their arrival in Calcutta, India, the Judsons met the famous English Baptist missionary William Carey and asked to be immersed (baptized by being put under the water). They were soon baptized at the Lal Bazaar Baptist Church. The Judsons followed what they felt God wanted, realizing they now had no support, because Baptists in America had not even organized as a denomination. Carey loaned them money to start their missions work in Burma and wrote to America to plead with Baptists to organize and support their new missionaries. Adoniram wrote as well.

The voyage to Burma was terrible, and when Ann and Adoniram arrived, they found a dirty, hot, and humid little city where no one spoke English. It was a shock. But God had made the perfect choice of His very first missionaries to go to Burma. Bad as things looked, Ann and Adoniram took courage and determined to share God's love in that land where no one even knew about the real God.

Adoniram was able to locate a scholar who agreed to teach them Burmese. *Maung Shwei Gnong* (Mohng Shway Nohng) was a brilliant man, and both Judsons learned quickly. (After a few years, their teacher, *Shwei Gnong* (Shway Nohng) personally put his faith in Christ and became a wonderful evangelist. He led many of his own people to know and love God.)

Adoniram studied ten hours a day, and Ann slightly less, because she needed to go to the market every day to buy food. She soon started wearing typical bright Burmese clothes. The tall, elegant foreign lady was popular in the marketplace. The people were fascinated by the beautiful foreigner who spoke fluent Burmese. Ann's heart hurt every day to realize these people didn't know that Creator God loved them personally. That made her even more determined to quickly learn Burmese so she could tell them.

Month after month, the young couple studied and learned. However, the Judsons were so very lonely. No one else spoke English. They wrote letters home, especially Ann, but mail took incredibly long to come and go. Finally, in September 1815, after three and a half years, they got their first letter from home. Ann was so excited that she couldn't even sleep that night!

Ann and Adoniram had church services together each Sunday, just the two of them. When they had the Lord's Supper, it was again just the two of them. Occasionally, they would weep a little and feel a bit forsaken. Yet in their hearts, they *knew* God was right there with them. They also knew they were where God wanted them to be.

Another night that Ann was too excited to sleep was the day the very first Burmese person, gentle *U Naw* (Ooh Nawh), came to trust Christ. This time they wept with joy. They had been in Burma six and a half years. Then *Maung Ing* (Mohng Eeng) the gentle fisherman, believed. Next was *Maung Shway Bay* (Mohng Shway Bay) who became an evangelist himself. Then the first woman, highly educated *Mah Men Lay* (Mah Mun Lay) trusted Christ. Within a year, there were twenty believers, and Ann and Adoniram rejoiced over each one.

That dreadful night of Adoniram's arrest, Ann felt too exhausted from weeping to sleep. All those memories kept coming through the darkness of the sleepless Ava night. Three years earlier, Ann had grown very ill with liver disease and there was no medical care. Ann recalled how God had been with them then. They were apart more than two years while Ann returned to America to find doctors who could help save her life. Remembering that, Ann realized again that God was *still* here with them. Adoniram might be in prison but the Lord would not desert them now in their time of great need. He had led them to endure sickness. Ann recalled how the Lord had allowed her to heal and for them to be together again and live here in the capital city of Ava.

Not only that: With God's help, Adoniram had just completed the translation of the entire New Testament. Soon, the people of Burma could read of God's love in their heart language. On that thought, fear clutched Ann's heart again. Her heart began thumping wildly. The precious New Testament! What would happen to it? The officials were bound to come search all their belongings. What if they found it and destroyed it? Gripped by anxiety, Ann realized she would get no sleep. This was like an endless nightmare. She fell to her knees again and prayed until dawn.

Morning finally arrived. Ann took a deep breath, then dressed in her brightest Burmese clothing. Wrapping herself in faith and courage, brave Ann Judson walked the two miles to the prison that stood right in the shadow of the emperor's palace. She must see what she could find out. She had to plan how to help her beloved Adoniram. She must keep him alive. He would be depending on her.

Ann could scarcely believe her eyes when she saw the filth and nasty conditions at the prison. Her cherished husband had always been fastidiously clean. Now Adoniram lay in all sorts of dirt and with fourteen pounds of fetters (iron chains) around his feet and hands. Prison filth was all over him. She took his hand, and whispered in his ear, "Take courage. God has not left us. He will help us through."

Ann Judson found a way to hide the New Testament manuscript. She also literally kept her husband alive for the twenty-two months he lay in two death prisons. Three different times the emperor ordered him executed. Each time, Ann persuaded the one kind official who had befriended her to please spare her husband's life. There was a presence about Ann Judson. Those fine eyes of hers seemed to be able to look into the heart of the one with whom she was talking. The official with a wise heart felt sorry for the gallant foreign lady who tried every day to help her husband. He pitied her and admired her bravery and courage.

Ann often saw despair written across Adoniram's face. She knew she had to be strong for his sake. Ann took him food every day and sometimes could bribe the greedy guards to let him spend some precious minutes each day in the sunshine of the courtyard. There, they could talk and pray together. The two of them somehow encouraged each other to bless God's name and take courage.

Some officials had no sympathy at all. It was as if they didn't have a heart. One especially hot day, Ann took her prized silk umbrella, a gift from a Burmese friend, to protect her head from the blazing sun while she walked the long, dusty road to an official's home. She was pleading for mercy for her husband. Maybe he would help. When Ann arrived, she had to wait in line another two hours just to be able to talk to him. Thank God for that umbrella to protect her from the boiling sun.

When the wicked official finally took the time to meet with her, she made her petition. He gave a little smirk and said, "No, no, I do not think there will be any favors granted to *foreigners* today." He refused to listen to her pleas. Her shoulders slumping, Ann drew a long breath and turned to leave. Suddenly, the wicked official called out, "Lady!" Ann quickly turned around, hoping he had somehow changed his mind. She looked at him expectantly. The official gave that same little smirk and reached out and grabbed her pink umbrella. Laughing, he exclaimed, "I like this lovely silk umbrella. I think I'll keep it. You are so thin the sun can't find you anyway!" And away he walked, leaving Ann with no protection from the sun and a heart heavy with unshed tears.

Realizing she would never forget that terrible moment at the door of the evil official, Ann walked the burning hot two miles back to their home. Unbidden tears ran down her cheeks the whole way. She dared not tell her husband about that official. Adoniram already felt terrible that he was helpless to come to her aid about anything.

By God's miraculous grace, the Judsons endured those twenty-two months. Adoniram was finally sent to write a peace treaty in both English and Burmese. No one else had that language ability. He was still under arrest at the time. Meanwhile, unknown to Adoniram, Ann lay close to death with a disease called spotted fever (spinal meningitis).

When Adoniram was finally set free and returned to their little home, he did not even recognize Ann. She lay motionless on their bed, so thin and emaciated that she did not even look like his beautiful Ann. He knelt beside the bed, weeping as he gazed at her thin face. Her eyes were closed as if asleep.

Maybe a stray tear fell on her cheek, for Ann opened her eyes, and looked wonderingly into the tear-filled eyes of her beloved. Radiant joy spread across her gaunt face and she reached up one thin hand to touch his cheek. Ann later wrote about that moment and how she had thought, *Is this a dream? Is it real? Is this really Adoniram, home at last?*

Now, for the first time in nearly two years, Adoniram could help Ann. With the aid of their faithful friend, and *Koochil*, the cook, Adoniram was able to nurse and care for her. Their friendly government official even took them to his home and helped provide nourishing food for Ann as she recuperated.

Three months later, the Judsons were completely free. They left Ava and went with the British forces, stopping at an encampment down the river. There, everyone waited for the British commandant and the Burmese ambassador to officially sign a treaty of peace. That treaty had been written by Adoniram Judson himself. The British officials and soldiers could not do enough for Ann. They honored her. All of them had heard the story of how she had saved her husband's life and how her heroism had made it possible for peace to finally become a reality.

That last night, a great banquet was held, where the British general hosted the Burmese army leaders and saw the treaty officially signed. The guest of honor that night was none other than beautiful Ann Judson, the hero of Ava. Lo and behold, there among the Burmese army delegation, sat the cruel official who had taken Ann's silk umbrella and left her to the mercy of the noonday sun. He looked up and saw Ann Judson. Immediately, his eyes grew wide with fear. He started trembling, and perspiration began running down his face.

Some of the British officers noticed the strange behavior of the Burmese delegate as they watched him looking fearfully at Ann Judson. His hand was shaking badly as he tried to raise a forkful of food to his lips. Ann pierced him with those fine eyes, and quietly said in Burmese, *"Gong Bah Deh. Gong Bah Deh"* (It is alright. It is alright). One of the British officers then turned to Ann and in a puzzled voice, asked, "What's going on? He seems very frightened."

Ann gave a little smile and calmly told the officers at the table the story of what had happened to her silk umbrella. The whole table of officers exclaimed and turned toward the Burmese official with anger written across their faces. Then Ann spoke once more to the trembling official, "You do not have to fear me." Surely God had given Ann sufficient grace to forgive a man who did not deserve it.

Adoniram chuckled that night when they got back to their tent. He felt a certain sense of satisfaction that Ann had been given such an opportunity to show grace in action. The newly freed couple felt as light as air. For the first time in two years, they were free! They could return to the work God had for them. Ann and Adoniram clasped hands and vowed again, "We will bless God and take courage."

The Rest of the Story

Ann Judson was exceedingly frail. She did not live long after Adoniram's release from prison. Although Ann's life was quite short, God used her in those fourteen years in Burma to change an entire nation. Furthermore, God used Ann to save the life of her husband. The priceless New Testament survived. Adoniram went on to translate the entire Bible into Burmese. That same translation is still in use. Today, there are more than four million Christians in Burma, a land with a population of only about fifty-nine million. Those Christians refer to themselves as spiritual descendants of the Judsons. The story of Ann and Adoniram Judson is the amazing and true account of God's miraculous power at work in two lives totally committed to Him.

Standing with Rosalie Hunt and Dr. Stanley Hanna, great-grandson of Ann and Adoniram Judson, at Ann's grave and monument are Joan Myint and Harriet Bain, great-great-granddaughters of Ah Vong, the Burmese-Chinese printer who published Judson's 1831 Bible translation.

Dr. Stanley Hanna, great-grandson of Adoniram Judson, with Rosalie Hunt in the archives of American Baptist Historical Society, examining the 1811 miniature of Adoniram Judson.

1845 portrait of Adoniram Judson

Chapter Four

Adoniram and the Priceless Pillow

Father was coming home tonight! Three-year-old Adoniram was brimming over with excitement. He had a big surprise for Father. Mother had helped him prepare the surprise, but he had mostly done it by himself. He kept running to the window every time he heard the *clop-clopping* of a horse going past their house. Finally, it was Father. Adoniram ran outside to welcome him home.

Rev. Adoniram Judson beamed when he saw his son and reached down to lift his little namesake into the saddle in front of him. After getting the horse settled down in the barn, the two went inside to the warmth of the fireplace and the hearty soup and cornbread Abigail Judson had waiting. The little fellow could scarcely contain his excitement, but Mother had told him to wait until Father had eaten before surprising him.

Rev. Judson was always quite dignified, but when it came to his son, his love and pride in this child was evident to all. Young Adoniram was standing by his father's knee when Mother spoke, "Son," she gently smiled, "why don't you show your father your surprise for him?"

Adoniram climbed onto his father's lap, and Mother handed him the family Bible. His father looked surprised to see his small son holding such a big book but watched indulgently as his child turned to Deuteronomy 5 and began reading the long chapter. Rev. Judson stared in amazement at his child. What on earth? A three-year-old reading like that? He was astonished and so very proud. Adoniram gazed at his father as, beaming from ear to ear, Rev. Judson spoke, his voice husky with emotion, "Son, my son, someday you will be a great man!" The young child never forgot his father's words. And sure enough, he did become a great man, but not in quite the way his father had imagined.

Abigail, his sister, was born when he was nearly three. She adored her big brother and followed him everywhere. Adoniram did everything quickly, and most of it with great ease. He had a boundless curiosity and wanted to explore anything new and intriguing. Throughout his school days, the young boy stood at the top of his class in all subjects. He was especially brilliant in languages.

Adoniram's father was a Congregational minister and changed pastorates several times during Adoniram's childhood. In 1802, the Congregational church in historic Plymouth, Massachusetts, split, and the new church immediately called Adoniram Judson Sr. as pastor. He bought property on the same street as the new church. The house was only about two blocks from Fort Hill, where the Pilgrims settled in 1620. In fact, the Judsons' new home was built on Watson's Hill, right where Chief Massasoit, Squanto, and Samoset camped during that first fateful winter. That was when the native Americans helped save the lives of the desperate Pilgrims.

Teenaged Adoniram became dangerously ill shortly after their move to Plymouth. He was close to death and was forced to spend more than a year in bed. The brilliant young man read and studied on his own and had plenty of time to daydream. Adoniram usually dreamed about himself as pastor of a large and influential church, preaching to masses of people who would hang on his every word. All the time, though, his heart told him that true greatness and rich rewards came in heaven, and to God the glory should be given. Many years later, he looked back at that very moment when his heart told him what was *really* important.

Adoniram's father, so proud of his son's brilliance, felt like conservative Brown University would be better for his son than Harvard University. A week after his sixteenth birthday, Adoniram was enrolled at Brown. Brown University's new student had pleasant features, striking chestnut hair, and large, hazel eyes. With his compelling bass voice and winsome personality, Adoniram quickly became popular on campus. Completing college in just three years, Adoniram Judson Jr. returned home in 1807 after graduating as valedictorian.

Strangely enough, this adult Adoniram was scarcely recognizable to his fond parents.

Brown University might have been conservative, but his studies and close friends were not necessarily conservative. Adoniram excelled in every class, but along the way he latched on to some very liberal ideas. His closest friend was Jacob Eames, a talented and witty fellow who was a Deist. Deists believed there was a God, but God was far removed from them, and they could succeed on their own intelligence. They didn't need God personally. When Adoniram's parents realized what his beliefs about Almighty God had become, they were shocked and saddened. There was no arguing with their son, however. He was a champion debater.

Adoniram taught school one year, then decided that wasn't for him. Off he went to New York, to see the big wide world, and maybe become a famous writer of theatrical productions. That ambition lasted about six weeks. Rather discouraged, Adoniram got on his horse and headed for home, not knowing quite what he wanted to do in life. His talents were many; the question was, what did he *really* want to do? To be?

Not far from Plymouth, a tired Adoniram stopped for the night in a small Massachusetts village. Asking the proprietor of the country inn for a room, the man replied, "Sorry, we have only one spare room and it is next to a young fellow who is very ill. I fear it would be a noisy and restless night." Adoniram shrugged and replied, "That is alright. I can sleep through anything. I'm very tired." Reluctantly, the innkeeper gave him a key to the room and up the stairs Judson went.

The innkeeper had been exactly right. It was a very long and noisy night. Just about the time Adoniram would doze off, there would be sounds from the next room — voices — footsteps — people hurrying in and out. And then, the occupant of the room would begin groaning. The groans and moans kept Adoniram unwillingly awake. Then, mixed in with the groaning, there were words; "Oh God, oh God," the voice would moan, and then again, in agony, "Oh God, lost. Lost. Lost."

The words were haunting. Sleepless, Adoniram lay there thinking, *Lost? Lost? What if that sick man was I? I'm lost. I have not trusted God.* Fear gripped his heart as the noises went on endlessly. He tossed and turned until, right before dawn, the sounds and the voice finally stopped. Adoniram drifted off into a weary sleep.

He woke up to bright sunlight streaming in his window. Getting up, Adoniram thought, *How foolish I was last night, to let the words of a stranger make me feel vulnerable. Here in the light of a bright day, I'm fine!*

With that thought, he briskly headed down to settle his charges. As he paid his bill, Adoniram cheerfully asked the innkeeper, "The fellow in the room next to me — did he finally get better?" Shaking his head, the man replied, "Oh no. He died toward morning. Say," the innkeeper asked, "didn't you tell me you went to Brown University?" When Adoniram nodded, the man continued, "The fellow in the room next to you went to Brown too. Eames. Jacob Eames. That was his name."

Adoniram stood there in shock. Jacob? His Deist friend who said he didn't need God? He was dead? And, as he died, he was calling out, "Lost. Lost."

As his horse clopped along the road toward Plymouth, Adoniram's mind and heart were in turmoil. For two whole weeks, Adoniram struggled and thought and walked and thought some more. Then, shocking his parents yet again, Judson announced, "I'm going to attend the new seminary in Andover."

Christ had turned Adoniram's life around. He came to salvation by confessing his sins and asking the Lord to enter his heart. Judson's parents found the profound and quick change in their son both amazing and wonderful. From that point on, their son's hopes and dreams all focused on serving God.

Adoniram enrolled at the seminary just weeks later. He was all in earnest. In a short time, Adoniram discovered there were three or four more students who felt as he did about serving God. Miraculously, God had placed in each of their hearts the needs of a world without hope. It was a world that needed someone to tell them about God and His love. The students formed a group and prayed together, searching for how God wanted them to literally go into the world. There were no missionaries from America to any nation or continent. How were they to go about this?

The group chose Adoniram as their spokesperson, and four of them walked together the nine miles to Bradford, where the Congregational church leaders were in annual meeting. They would seek help. And that week, the very first missionary sending group in America was organized. Furthermore, that was the same notable day when Adoniram Judson first saw beautiful Ann Hasseltine and fell in love. In less than two years, they married and set sail for the Far East, eager to discover what God had in mind for them.

Adoniram had always loved languages. As he studied and prayed, he became convinced that Bible translation was what God wanted him to do. There were nations who had no Bible in their heart language. One of these was Burma, in the same part of the world as India, where English Baptists had recently begun work. The remarkable William Carey had, just a short time before, translated the Bible into the language of India. Burma had no Scripture at all in the Burmese language. This was a challenge, and Judson loved challenges.

Having realized that they needed to be immersed (baptized) as Jesus was, Ann and Adoniram were baptized in India. They headed by faith to Burma, praying that Baptists in America would organize and support them. After reaching Burma, they quickly realized the challenges were great. There were no believers; there was no one who spoke English. Ann and Adoniram had many lonely months of studying and preparing themselves to share the gospel news with the people of Burma.

More than three years passed before they received the glad letters holding good news: Baptists in their homeland were now organized and were supporting the Judsons as their very first missionaries! In the same mail came letters from home — the first they had received since they had left Salem, Massachusetts, so long before.

The great news gave fresh courage to their hearts. Both Judsons were inspired to study even harder and translate Scripture into the Burmese language so the people could read for themselves how God loved them. They desperately needed to know He had provided a way to give them eternal life.

Just five days after the wonderful mail arrived from America, a beautiful baby boy was born to Ann. Little Roger was the joy of their hearts. However, only eight months later, joy turned to grief when their precious baby came down with a strange fever. Within three days, little Roger drew his last breath, and his parents wept many tears. The light of their hearts had gone out. But God was their comfort and help, and they determined to go on doing the work God had called them to. Their task was hard, so very hard. They must take courage.

First, one of them would be sick, then the other. Adoniram had a terrible time with his eyesight and some days could not even stand light in his eyes. How could he study and translate Scripture? He would rest and rest, and then start back again. Ann had repeated problems with liver disease. She would lose weight and be in pain, and then one time she had to go to India to find a doctor to help.

Still, they studied and learned, translated and prayed. Late at night, they would encourage each other. Adoniram would say, "My love, we must battle on, somehow we must." And Ann would respond, "We will, my dear husband; we will *not* give up. God will help us to bless His name and take courage." On that comforting thought, they would fall asleep.

Ann and Adoniram kept faithfully on, studying, praying, fighting the diseases that invaded their bodies. And sometimes, they would just take a deep breath and remind each other, "God is with us. He will not fail us. He sent us here." Six years passed before the first Burman believed in Christ and was baptized. That night, the Judsons were the most excited and happy people in all of Burma. God had given them fruit!

Sure enough, life was never easy and smooth. Adoniram left on a simple voyage to Chittagong, India, where there were Christians. He went to find a Christian scholar who could help in translating the Bible. One catastrophe after another hit, typhoons nearly destroyed the ship and Adoniram came perilously close to death from sickness. A simple four-week trip became seven grueling months of danger.

Ann held the mission together back home. After Adoniram returned, however, she became deathly ill with liver disease. To save her life, Ann was forced to sail to America for doctors and medicine. Adoniram was determined, and he took courage and somehow persevered without his beloved Ann. They were apart for more than two years before he had the matchless joy of seeing Ann arrive on a ship from America. What excitement they felt! Adoniram had just completed the translation of the New Testament into Burmese, and now, Ann was home again.

The two of them went to Ava, the capital city, to work and translate. They hoped to win the emperor's favor for Christians. Alas, ominous trouble loomed. England was close to war with Burma, and the emperor was very suspicious of all foreigners, calling them spies. Sure enough, in June 1824, the prison guards came and dragged Adoniram to the death prison. It stood right in the shadow of the palace and was deathly feared by everyone.

Somehow, Adoniram lived through nearly two years, bound and shackled, in two different prisons. His beloved Ann kept him alive by taking him food every day. Adoniram feared for the safety of the newly translated Burmese New Testament. What if the government found the Scripture and destroyed ten years of work?

However, when Ann went to the prison, she whispered to Adoniram about the plan she was devising. She took the priceless New Testament translation, rolled it as tightly as she could, and covered it in thin cotton. Then putting on another layer of cloth and then another, she began making a lacquer covering. The bundle was long, and in the shape of a Burmese pillow. The usual Burmese pillow was hard. This pillow she made, with its many layers of lacquer, was certainly hard as well.

The Judsons knew the Burmese people loved bribes. That was a way to earn extra money. Ann learned during those two years to bribe and then bribe again, so she could get some help for her Adoniram. That bright morning, when she first took the lacquer "pillow" to the prison, she bribed the guard. Sure enough, he allowed the prisoner to use the hard pillow, never knowing that it contained the priceless Word of God.

Not long after Adoniram was thrown into prison, Ann gave birth to a tiny baby girl. Adoniram would never forget his first sight of his precious little daughter. Ann brought her to the prison to meet her daddy for the first time. He wept bitter tears because he was a prisoner, and absolutely helpless to do anything to help his wife or baby. Ann saw the agony written on his face. She bent near and whispered, "Adoniram, God is still with us. Bless God and take courage." Just hearing those words from his courageous wife strengthened the heart and faith of this man lying helpless in a death prison.

More trouble loomed. The foreign prisoners were moved to yet *another* terrible prison. They were allowed to take nothing with them. Adoniram and Ann wept bitter tears. The priceless New Testament manuscript was gone forever. Somehow, Adoniram vowed, he must survive so he could translate it again.

After what seemed like a lifetime, word spread that a peace treaty was being talked about. Judson was the only man in all Burma who was an expert at both Burmese and English. He was still under guard, as it took days and weeks to write up a treaty. Judson had no way of knowing his adored Ann had become ill with the deadly spotted fever. It killed nearly everyone who became infected with the disease.

But God worked another miracle. Adoniram was finally released, only to walk into their little house and find Ann on her bed, looking more dead than alive. Now, for the first time in two years, he could do something for *her*. She was the one who had kept him fed and alive for two years. Now was his chance to minister to her needs.

Slowly, very slowly, Ann began to regain strength. One morning, their friend *Maung Ing* (Mohng Eeng) came to them holding something that looked old and tattered in his hands. He smiled and held it out to Adoniram, quietly speaking, "Honored teacher, the day they took you to the second prison, I went to the old prison, just to look and see if there was anything of yours." He shyly explained, "I just wanted to have anything that would remind me of my wonderful teacher. I found this. This is what was left of your pillow." He looked apologetic as he added, "I know it looks dirty. The guards had torn the pretty lacquer covering off. But I thought you might want it anyway."

Ann and Adoniram stared at the tattered cloth remaining around the core of the pillow. Wonder dawned in their eyes, as they realized what Adoniram was actually holding — the entire Burmese New Testament. Miraculously, it had been preserved, right under the eyes of the enemy guards. Their dear friend *Maung Ing* (Mohng Eeng) was the instrument God used to rescue His word. The Judsons began to weep tears of joy. So did their friend when he realized that the tattered bundle was actually God's holy Word.

Ann recovered, and the Judsons went with the British army as they left Ava and headed to the south of Burma to possess the land there. In the British-occupied area, people were free and cared for. Ann and Adoniram were thrilled to be able to preach and teach again, and work with the band of believers who had survived the war.

The Judsons set out afresh as a team to begin preaching and teaching. The believers were so excited to be able to meet and worship together once more. All of them now had freedom to tell the good news. The Judsons continually blessed God and took courage. It was as if their lives and ministry had been handed back to them.

The situation did not remain calm and encouraging, however. Within a few months, Adoniram was asked to write another treaty with a clause that religious liberty would be guaranteed. He did not want to leave at all, but Ann urged him, saying, "Adoniram, if religious liberty is written in, it will be worth the effort!" Ann seemed well now, so very reluctantly Judson left to work on the treaty.

One night, quite unexpectedly, Ann's fever returned. It wasn't bad at first, but then, each day it got worse, and she soon realized the deadly spotted fever had returned. British doctors worked tirelessly to save her life. Ann had lost so much strength during the terrible prison years that her frail body could not fight off the dreaded disease. The evening of that last day, Ann whispered, "The teacher (Adoniram) is long in coming." Her last words were in Burmese, now the language of her heart. Until the very end, the heart of this courageous woman maintained its deep faith and commitment. She was faithful to the words that most illustrated her heart and bravery: *We will bless God and take courage.*

The Rest of the Story

Ann Judson was only thirty-six when she died, but her gift of love and bravery impacted and changed an entire nation. She forever became "Mama Judson" to the believers in Burma. Adoniram grieved for many years. However, he did not stop working and preaching and translating. Judson translated the entire Bible into Burmese, and it is still the most perfect translation over two hundred years later.

Adoniram married again and preached and taught until his death in 1850. God used that remarkable man to bring the good news to the people of Burma, instilling hope where there had been no hope. Two of his grandchildren became missionaries to Burma and carried on the Judson legacy. And to this day, in the villages, cities, and countryside of Burma, parents tell the story of *Yoodthan* (Adoniram) and Ann and how they brought the gospel story to Burma. Adoniram Judson left all believers a wonderful statement that reflects his great faith and optimistic spirit. He was often asked, "What do you think about the future of missions?" He always responded with great hope, "It is as bright as the promises of God."

1823: Sketch of Let Ma Yoon Prison at Ava, where Adoniram Judson lay in fourteen pounds of fetters.

*Bleak Hall, Edisto Island, South Carolina —
home of Hephzibah Jenkins Townsend.*

Chapter Five

Hephzibah Jenkins Townsend Tells Her Own Story

I wish I could have known my mother. She was Hephzibah, too — Hephzibah Frampton Jenkins of Edisto Island, South Carolina. Daniel Jenkins, my father, was a captain with the Revolutionary Army. He was stationed in Charleston, so Mama took my little brother Daniel to stay with relatives while she went to Charleston to be with Father. She wanted him to be with her when I was born.

But this was May 1780. The British laid siege to Charleston and Father was captured. So, it was just Mama and Maum Jean and Jack, our trusted servants, at our house on Calhoun Street. At night, they all stayed in the basement because they wanted no lantern lights to show. It was too dangerous.

Mama was very frail and expecting a baby (me) at any moment. Maum Jean and Jack had been with Mama since she was a little girl. They cared for her so tenderly. I was born that Wednesday night, May 10, 1780 — and just two days later, Charleston fell into the hands of the British. Now no one dared appear in the streets.

Mama told Maum Jean and Jack, "I'm naming my baby Hephzibah, for this Bible name means 'My delight is in her.' It also means one who is guarded and protected. God knows my baby needs protecting. Promise me," she pleaded with them, "you will take her home to Edisto. Guard her with your lives. And tell my little boy his mama loves him."

Oh Miss Hephzibah," Maum Jean pleaded, "please hold on; you are going to make it." But Mama knew she was dying. She was only nineteen years old. That Monday night, Mama breathed her last. Dear Jack emptied a large trunk from the attic and lined it with a soft quilt. They tenderly put Mama in it and by moonlight, buried her in the backyard.

Then they got ready to take me to safety. Jack had a little rowboat hidden in the reeds on the river, and Maum Jean made little pacifiers of sugar and butter. She wrapped them in soft linen and used them to try to keep me quiet as they escaped Charleston.

It took four days and nights to get to Edisto. They could only travel those forty miles at night. They hid during the day. Maum Jean later told me that I was so tiny, so frail, that "by the time we got you home, Honey, you were about only fit for the fishes!"

But they made it — and because of them, I lived. I always knew I must be "fit" for something special — why else would God have spared my life? I realized as just a little child that God had something *special* for me to do. His hand was upon me, for surely I was bought with a price. From my mama, I inherited the large plantation area named Bleak Hall.

When I was about a month old, Father was released from the British prison. He grieved over the loss of his beloved Hephzibah, but he was so glad that I survived, thanks to Maum Jean and Jack. Father later remarried distant cousin Martha Seabrook. They had seven children, so I had half brothers and sisters.

My baby sister, Amarinthia, was born when I was ten, and I felt like a little mother to her. We had a very special bond all our lives. We did many things together. Amarinthia became a charter member with me of a very important group of women. And she helped me start a church!

When I was a young girl, I loved trips to Charleston to see our relatives there. Father was an Episcopalian, but many of our Charleston kinfolk were Baptist. They were a big influence on me. Most Edisto Island people were Presbyterian or Episcopal, but I wasn't exactly like most of the others. I had "Baptist leanings"! I do know that long ago, there had been several Baptists on Edisto, and a little church too. Rev. William Screven of Charleston used to come to Edisto to preach back in the early 1700s.

Those were special childhood days. Edisto is a beautiful spot. I loved the tall, live oaks. They just drip with moss, and at night the owls call to one another from tree to tree. Oh my, when the flowers were in full bloom, home was like walking in a wonderland.

My closest friend and companion was my brother Daniel. He was only two when I was born, and we always had a special bond. Brother and I loved Christmastime. All the big plantations would come together and have a giant outdoor celebration, with venison, barbecued wild boar, oysters, and terrapin stew. We'd have mince pies and sweet potato puddings. It lasted all day and was never to be forgotten.

I learned early how to read and write, and how to direct a household. After all, I was the oldest daughter, and the family depended on my domestic skills. Our family plantations were quite extensive and all of us were busy. Of course, slavery was part of our culture. But I couldn't look at slavery like our family and friends did. You see, Maum Jean and Jack had saved my life. Literally. They were my people, my family.

Edisto had several large plantations, so we had neighbors. Most of them were relatives, one way or another. Cousins married cousins, and we were careful who we talked about — they were kin to nearly everyone else! Our close neighbors were the Townsends. They were also distant relatives, and we saw a lot of them.

The Townsends' son, Daniel Townsend III, was much older than I. In fact, he was twenty-one when I was born. Actually, my great-grandfather Townsend was Daniel's *grandfather*. Daniel was always kind to me. When I was twelve, he told my father he was just "waiting for me to grow up."

He waited until I was nearly fifteen when he proposed. Daniel told me he admired "my quiet dignity, my sense of justice, and my force of character." (About a dozen years later, I wondered what he thought *then* about my force of character!) We were married on April 9, 1796, one month before my sixteenth birthday.

You understand, of course, that in those days, when a woman married, her property moved under the control of her husband. That made for some interesting discussions! Some young brides could handle that custom very easily. I was not one of those.

We began building our home, Bleak Hall — it was a huge undertaking. My brother Daniel had not married yet, and he lived with us, even though Shargould was his property. He became a beloved uncle to our little children. There were plenty of them to love! I gave birth to fifteen children. Our first two little sons only lived one year. Then John Ferrars was born, a strong, healthy boy. However, we then lost two more sons before Mary Frampton was born in 1804 — and she thrived.

However, tragedy hit that same year. My beloved brother took his new boat for an outing. My two half-brothers and several friends went as well. A sudden squall hit, and only one of the twelve survived. Now my closest friend on earth was gone.

Brother had made me his heir, so his plantation, Shargould, came to me. In just a few years, that would become very important. When I was a young teenager, I came to realize the lost-ness of my soul. My only hope was in Christ. So, I asked Him into my heart, never having forgotten how He had made it possible for me to survive. I knew I was sinner, so I accepted His gift of eternal life and asked Him into my heart. Now I was a sinner saved by grace.

My husband was active in the Presbyterian church, but I never really felt at home there. Occasionally, Dr. Richard Furman, of First Baptist Church Charleston, came to Edisto to preach. That was always the highlight of the month. He was the most famous Baptist minister in America.

I began going to Charleston on Sundays to attend services at First Baptist Church there. The rowing trip took six hours each way, but that gave me a lot of time to think and pray. I could meditate on what my service for God should be. Then in 1807, I was baptized by Dr. Furman. That made my heart so happy.

Those were busy years, raising children and running a plantation. Traveling a long distance to church took a lot of time. All those years, I longed to have a Baptist church here on Edisto, so we could worship at home. The busier I became, the more difficult travel grew to be.

In those Sunday services, I learned of the world's need to hear about Christ. So many people around the world had never even heard the name "Jesus." Then in 1810, I learned from Pastor Furman about a special group of women up in Boston. Polly Webb, a young disabled woman, organized some ladies to pray and give to missions. They formed a female mite society.

Dr. Furman also told me about William Carey and the beginning of missions work in India. It hit me with real force. Here I was on this safe little island, but half a world away were millions of people who had never had a chance to hear about the creator God who loved them. The Great Commission suddenly became *real* to me. What could "I" do? And the seed of an idea was born in my mind and heart.

I had to talk to my dear sister, Amarinthia, about this. She always had good ideas. I knew it would be no easy task — but it might work! The very next morning, I got in the buggy and made the trip to Amarinthia's home. She was excited about my plans. The two of us then went together to see several of our friends. If women like Polly in Boston could serve the Lord, surely God could use women on Edisto Island too!

What about having our *own* female mite society? Well, it would take money. I had funds, but I had no control over those funds! You see, my husband was a staunch Presbyterian elder. I did approach him. I said, "My dear, I need money for Dr. William Carey and missions causes." Well, he was *not* interested in causes half a world away. He refused to allow me to have money. I was most unhappy. I fretted a bit and prayed a lot. I also knew so clearly that Scripture tells us: "To whom much is given, of him shall much be required."

So, I asked again — and again. No change. Alright. I knew that now was the time for action. The next week, I sent my servant, Bella, who was also my dear friend, to Charleston. She was a wonderful cook. I sent her to the leading pastry chef in Charleston. He trained her in specialty baking. Her very best item was gingerbread that melted in your mouth. Bella was so talented.

Next, I had some outdoor ovens constructed of tabby. Tabby is a strong type of cement made from crushed oyster shells and lime. In those ovens, we baked wonderful gingerbread and specialty cakes.

To this day, I can still inhale the aroma of that hot gingerbread baking in those tabby ovens! And that was the beginning of our "missions business." My plan was to bake during the week and take the goods to Charleston on Saturdays. I would sell them at the Charleston market.

My husband had a fit. He wasn't going to let *his* farmhands spend all day each Saturday in Charleston. "Alright!" I told Daniel. "I'll take the gingerbread and sell it myself." Now Daniel was a dignified man. His pride certainly couldn't take his *wife* selling gingerbread in the market.

So, he relented. The sales began, and the Wadmalaw-Edisto Female Mite Society was born.

We ladies met at Bleak Hall, and each lady found a way to make her own unique contribution. We prayed together for missionaries in other lands. At the end of that first year, in 1811, our offering totaled $122.50. That was a lot of gingerbread! Folks on Edisto began calling me "the Gingerbread Lady." The truth was that our dear Maum Bella was the *real* gingerbread lady. She was a wizard at baking!

Then in 1813, Luther Rice came to Charleston. I was able to meet him. He told me about Ann and Adoniram Judson. I learned that they were Baptists now and were missionaries in faraway Burma. Our little mite society assured Mr. Rice that money would be coming from us for the Judsons' work.

Sure enough, when Baptists got together to form into a denomination the next year, 1814, the only society in the South to have a donation listed at that meeting was ours — the Wadmalaw-Edisto Female Mite Society.

But Edisto needed a church as well as a missionary society, so I began catering for island parties and weddings. I guess that meant I was the first businesswoman on Edisto. But this was the Lord's business. And by 1818, the church was built. I gave the land and property permanently to the church. Most of the members were enslaved people. But I was part of these people. My heart was here.

In only one church on Edisto Island could enslaved people have a *voice* and know they were equal and part of the church leadership. This was at Edisto Baptist. There was one special person who made that church a reality. That was our beloved Maum Bella. Her love for the Lord and her wonderful baking made the Edisto Baptist Church possible. And our church grew to 450 members.

However, just about this time, I had a crisis in our home. Daniel was preparing his will. He decided he wanted to follow the British custom of inheritance. That meant everything would basically go to the eldest son. But I had a big problem with that. We had many beloved children. What about *them*?

Our disagreements were *very* sharp. Finally, I simply and quietly moved out of our house. I went to Shargould, the property my brother had willed to me. I had a house constructed there. Those were not easy days. However, I had a deep conviction that this was something I must do.

My dear Daniel finally came to my way of thinking. He rewrote his will to include all our children. And I moved back to Bleak Hall! I must say this about my dear husband — in spite of his stubbornness, he always came around to mending fences with me.

The culture of my day called a man "weak" if he listened to his wife. But that dear man honestly did respect my force of character and sense of justice. Daniel even joined me in working with lawyers to make *sure* our Baptist church property was safe for the people of the church. That way, no one could ever take it away.

I recall we had a wonderful experience the week of Christmas, 1844. We had "special meetings" every night from December 21st to the 26th. We met in my parlor at Bleak Hall, and I assisted Pastor McDunn in the services. We would start at about seven in the evenings and never finished before midnight. Praise God, over sixty souls were born into God's kingdom. We baptized all of them at the end of that week.

Our mite society continued to add projects to help people. We loved to pray together and to give to missions. We used the missionary magazine to learn about what was happening overseas. We were shocked to learn our missionaries, the Judsons, were enduring war and prison. All of us prayed earnestly that they would be spared. They were released after about two years.

I have been so blessed. Daniel lived to be 83. We managed to weather the storms of life together. Furthermore, I had the joy of our special church. The mite society was also a great blessing in my life. Would you believe, the idea of missionary societies began to spread. I lived to see them in many towns in South Carolina and other states too.

These later years of my life, I think so often about Maum Jean and Jack. I think how God used them to save my life. I think about how God called me and gave me so many opportunities to serve Him. And every day I remember: I am just a sinner saved by grace.

Sometimes I wish I could see into the many years to come. I wish I could tell the believers then how it is worth it all, just to serve God. It is such joy to serve such a Savior. And I think about the Bible name my mother gave me — Hephzibah ("my delight is in her"). I pray that when I get to heaven, I can hear our Savior say, "Hephzibah, well done, well done. My delight is in you."

The Rest of the Story

Hephzibah Jenkins Townsend can be called the "Mother" of Woman's Missionary Union. All the little mite societies in all the states banded together to form a national organization. And it all began with a little woman named Hephzibah on a small island in South Carolina who had a vision of what God could do with a "sinner saved by grace." As a young woman, she determined to follow that vision.

Her dear Maum Bella was offered her freedom from slavery. Bella did not accept it, but she did accept it for her son, Lewis. Lewis became a prosperous builder and businessman in Charleston.

The church that Hephzibah founded celebrated its 200th anniversary in 2018. They built a new structure next to the 1818 building. It was packed that anniversary day. And they all honored Hephzibah Jenkins Townsend — who, like they, was just a sinner saved by grace.

Tabby ovens where Hephzibah's gingerbread was baked — 1847.

Edisto Baptist Church, founded by Hephzibah Jenkins Townsend — 1818, Edisto Island, South Carolina.

Grave and monument to Hephzibah Jenkins Townsend — 1847.

*Annie Armstrong portrait
(Courtesy of Woman's Missionary Union)*

Chapter Six

Annie at Home on the Range

Annie Armstrong sat tall in the saddle, all six feet of her. She was a striking sight, her dark brown hair braided and worn like a crown under her hat, and her black riding habit getting dustier by the mile. She and Anna Schimp were riding in companionable silence, broken occasionally by a comment on the scenery or an idea of what might be beyond the mountain range ahead.

Years earlier, Anna Schimp and her husband had immigrated to America from Switzerland. Sadly, her husband died. Anna was left a wealthy widow, one who loved God. Her great wish was for people who had never heard about a Savior to learn of His love, so she joined Woman's Missionary Union.

The leader of that organization, Annie Armstrong, had become her friend. Anna was thrilled to be Miss Annie's traveling companion and accompany her on long mission trips. She, like Miss Annie, loved to be on the open range. It felt free and challenging. Clear blue skies, distant hills, and space as far as you could see were exhilarating.

Annie smiled at her companion, "Have you ever seen so much dust in one place as on this trail on an Indian reservation?" Mrs. Schimp shook her head as she responded, "I surely haven't, and never before have I *eaten* dust as we seem to be doing!" Annie Armstrong chuckled and remarked, "If it isn't a herd of buffalo passing by and raising the dust, it is our two horses creating a dust storm of their own!"

Annie continued, "I have been humming a new tune, Anna, one I learned just a few months ago — 'Home on the Range.'" Annie smiled, "The words are so true when I sing about the place 'where the deer and the antelope play, and the skies are not cloudy all day.' And here we are, out on the range!" She waved one arm in a wide gesture.

"Anna, I must tell you, my favorite place to visit is surely the reservations here in Oklahoma," Annie commented. "I wonder what Mother, back in Baltimore, would think if she could see her youngest daughter right now, riding across the wide-open prairie all covered with dust and the temperatures reaching 108?"

Miss Armstrong had a special love for Native Americans and their territory in Oklahoma ever since her first trip in 1900. She spent forty days on that journey and traveled over 4,000 miles. Annie smiled to herself as she recalled that first trip. Twenty years earlier, when Annie was in her early twenties, Cousin Eugene Levering was the sponsor of the Levering Manual Labor School for Native American boys in the town of Wetumpka. Annie and her friends in their Home Mission Society (of which Annie was the president) had volunteered to sew a whopping 240 summer suits for the boys in the school. Ever since then, Oklahoma held a special corner of her heart.

She and her friend listened to the rhythmic *clop, clop, clop* of their horses' hooves as they headed to their next meeting. Annie's mind drifted back through the years to her earliest memories. Thirty years earlier, young Annie in Baltimore, Maryland, could never have imagined traveling all this distance. This was like experiencing a different world. Annie silently thanked God for giving her such unique opportunities to help others. She felt like she was doing something to make an eternal difference for people who knew nothing about God's love.

Annie sighed and thought even *further* back to 1852. She was just two years old when her dear father, James Armstrong, had died very suddenly. Her mother, Mary Elizabeth, was left alone with four children and another on the way. Mary Armstrong was the strongest, most courageous woman Annie had ever known, and she loved her fiercely.

Sister Alice was four years older and was the dearest friend and companion Annie had her whole life. Both young Armstrong girls were tall, regal, brilliant, and committed to loving and helping others. Even as a young girl, Annie wanted to be a businesswoman. She felt like she would be good at that. Many a time she regretted being a female and not having the liberty to explore her talents in business like men did. (Sure enough, God did use those skills and talents of Annie's when she became the first leader of a remarkable organization for women.)

Neither sister married although they had beaus aplenty. When Annie was about thirty, a distinguished missionary from China visited Baltimore. His wife had died the year before and left him with four children. He wanted to return to China as soon as possible, and he wanted to marry and have a mother for his children. Fifteen years older than Annie Armstrong, the gentleman was highly impressed by her abilities and her love for missions. In a short time, he proposed to the regal young Annie.

Telling him she needed time to consider the proposal, Annie thought deeply and prayed earnestly about what she should do. She knew she loved missions and wanted to spend her life sharing God's message. Could his plan be for her to go to China? Over and over the thought came to Annie: *I am gifted as a businesswoman, and I can use this ability to spread the gospel. However, I am not skilled at languages. I simply do not have that gift.* Quietly but firmly, Annie gave her answer to the missionary. She was honored, but she must decline.

The Baltimore in which the Armstrong children grew up was a little piece of the whole world, with its fine harbor and hundreds of thousands of immigrants coming to its shores from all *over* the world. Annie's friend Anna Schimp was one of those. Anna was now an American, and she loved to secretly give her money to help missions causes. She didn't want others to know about her contributions, so Miss Annie honored that wish.

As the sun beat down and the clouds of dust on the reservation showed no signs of letting up, Annie turned to her companion, saying, "Did I ever tell you about *our* family of immigrants?" Anna looked surprised and responded with a puzzled frown, "I didn't know your family also immigrated!" Miss Annie grinned, "Oh, yes. My great-great-grandfather, Henry Sater, was born in England and came to the New World in 1709, when he was just 19. He was fifty when he married Dorcas Towson, my great-great-grandmother."

Anna Schimp loved hearing about Annie's family and the long ago. She listened intently as Miss Annie told of her Baptist beginnings. "There were no Baptist churches back then," explained Annie. "Only itinerant preachers who came through occasionally. They traveled and preached from one village to another.

"Henry and Dorcas were Baptists, and they gave the land on which a little church was constructed," she continued. "So the first Baptist church in Maryland was built there at Chestnut Ridge. It was soon named Sater's Baptist Church." Annie's eyes crinkled in a smile as she told her friend, "Every year we have what is called Cherry Sunday, and our kinfolk from all over return to Sater's Baptist Church to celebrate. I love to go."

Annie continued, "When I was a little girl, my first thing to do when arriving at the church was to climb up in one of the beautiful cherry trees. I'd plop a ripe red cherry in my mouth! Watching all the relatives arrive in their buggies was always fun. Some I knew, and a lot I didn't.

All of us worshipped and sang and studied the Bible and learned Baptist history. Then," Annie paused significantly, "we had a splendid dinner on the grounds. All the relatives brought baskets full of food. Oh my, all the pies and cakes and fried chicken. Wonderful!" Her friend grinned, "Please stop! You are making me hungry!"

"Well," Annie told her, her mind back to the present, "we will likely be eating very *different* food this evening on the Sac and Fox reservation." Anna Schimp quickly responded, "It will be a treat for me. I have never had such an exciting adventure as this." Looking around her at the rolling plains and tall grass waving back and forth in the scorching heat, she added, "Nor have I ever been so hot! Thank goodness for these hats with brims. When I was growing up, I wore head wraps to keep out the *cold* as I walked through the heavy snow in Switzerland!"

Anna Schimp was curious, "Please tell me, Miss Annie, how you became interested in missions." Annie Armstrong smiled and recalled, "One of my earliest memories was of our church, Seventh Avenue Baptist. Then our church sponsored a new congregation closer to our home, and we became charter members at Eutaw Baptist Church." Annie laughed and added, "I used to say that I *might* be a Presbyterian, or maybe an Episcopalian, but *never* a Baptist!"

Then Annie got serious and explained to her friend, "About that time, the Civil War came close to tearing our nation apart. It was especially awful in Baltimore because Maryland was a border state. Half of the people sympathized with the North and the others with the South." Annie took another breath and, shaking her head back and forth, added, "I simply couldn't find peace. I talked to Pastor Fuller about it. War was swirling all around and I longed for peace. One Sunday, Dr. Fuller explained in his sermon, "What the Christian has is not peace *from* trouble, but peace *in the midst* of trouble." And that was the day I completely gave myself to Christ. I asked Him to give me that peace that comes from trusting Him as Savior. And then," Annie concluded, "I knew I wanted to wholeheartedly serve Him and be what He wanted me to be."

By this time, Annie and Anna had arrived at the reservation. On this reservation were several believers, and there was great curiosity about the "tall white woman who walked in the Jesus way." People in the tribe seldom saw anyone like Annie Armstrong. They had never seen a stately white lady standing six feet tall. She visited in numerous tepees and was warmly welcomed each time. The bright eyes of the children sparkled as they noticed the tall white visitor had to bend down to enter the tepee.

That evening, both Annie and Anna were greeted with huge smiles. Each woman very solemnly came forward to greet them with three handshakes, the tribal way of expressing friendship. The women who were believers were enthusiastic about organizing a missionary society. Annie was elated that they wanted to be part of God's plan to help their own sisters as well as the world they had never visited.

Annie's trips out West were uncomfortable, difficult, exhausting, and exhilarating. She wished she had the time to spend five years on the frontier. That way, she felt she could lead and organize those women into a strong force for missions. It was so frustrating not to have the time or freedom to do just that. God had work for her back East as well as across the nation. Miss Annie was determined to fulfill her calling.

Anna Schimp was curious as to how Annie became head of WMU. So, on the trip back East, Annie told her missions story. "Mother was my example of the kind of strong and courageous woman I longed to be. It was like our name should be turned around, for I needed to have a 'strong arm.'" Annie smiled, "You see, Mother became a charter member of the group called Woman's Mission to Woman. They were organized by Mary Baker Graves. She was such an amazing woman,"

Annie recalled. "Her son, Roswell Graves, was a missionary doctor to South China, and he did wonderful work there. I was in awe of him," Annie remembered.

Roswell told his mother that the women of China needed to hear the gospel. However, in that country men could not talk with strange women, so it must be other *women* who could tell them about God's love. Dr. Graves knew that Christian Chinese women could go from home to home and tell the good news. Of course, money was needed to send them.

Annie paused to catch her breath. "So that is why those women organized in Baltimore, to raise funds to send Bible women from house to house to tell Chinese women about God." Annie smiled at the memory, "I was about eighteen then. Mother kept our little mite box on the breakfast table. Every week," she told Mrs. Schimp, "we each put in two pennies to help fill the box. Then all the money in all the little mite boxes was collected and sent to China so Bible women there could tell of Jesus' love."

Anna Schimp smiled as she thought of the strong WMU organization Miss Armstrong was now leading. Women and children all over America were giving money and gifts so people in many countries could hear the gospel. Annie happily told her friend the story of those early years and the challenge to organize. "Anna," she shook her head in disbelief, "would you believe, one of our biggest problems was the Baptist *men* who were leaders? Lots of them worried that women would want to just take over and become the leaders. But that was not what happened at all," Annie assured her friend. "We simply wanted to do our part and answer God's call to go and tell. Our idea was to work *with* the men. That is exactly what we have ended up doing."

When a weary Annie returned to Baltimore, Mother and Alice were thrilled at her stories about the West. Within just a day, however, she was back at her desk, working day and night.

About two years later, Mrs. Schimp was elated when Annie Armstrong invited her to return to the West with her. The plan was for them to visit pastors and their families *who were* doing pioneer work on the western frontier. In addition, much of their time would be spent on several reservations. On the second day of their long train trip to the frontier, Anna asked, "Miss Annie, please tell me more about the start of our missions organization. I wish I could have been in on the beginning," she smiled wistfully.

Annie sat a little straighter in her train seat as she reminisced. "Actually," Annie related, "Mrs. Graves started getting women together informally each year when the Baptist convention met. This started back in 1868 when I was just eighteen." Annie thought a moment and added, "For years, Lottie Moon had been writing to us from China, urging us to organize so we could do more by working together. So Baptist women in Maryland began planning about *how* to organize. Other states wanted this as well." Annie paused before adding, "We had informal gatherings each May during the convention. Finally, in 1887, we agreed to try to *officially* organize the next year."

Miss Annie smiled at the memory. "Sister Alice has been my greatest helper all these years. She is the writer. Oh my, can she write!" Annie said, "I recall that Alice prepared a paper on organizing and read it to the women when we met in 1888, in Richmond, Virginia. Our friend from South Carolina, Fannie Stout, also read an excellent paper encouraging women to organize."

Annie's face was alight as she continued, "And organize we did! On May 14, 1888, we became Woman's Missionary Union, Auxiliary to the Southern Baptist Convention." Anna Schimp beamed with pleasure as she exclaimed, "Now see how God has blessed this work! I am so happy to be part of such a union. Exhausted but happy!"

Miss Annie nodded, "It was like a cherished dream come true, and not just for me, but for all our women. Lottie Moon had been telling me for at least five years that Methodist and Presbyterian women organized a long time ago. Their work was strong and growing. And *that* was because they organized and worked together."

Annie smiled at Anna, "Women pulling together get a lot more done than by working just one on one. I'm so glad that Miss Moon pushed us to come together as a union. And now look. See how much more we are accomplishing! It is like I so often say to our women: 'Go Forward.' In fact," Annie grinned and inquired, "I wonder if you have noticed the sign over my desk in the office. It reads 'Go Forward.'" Annie stopped, then added, "Anna, that is what I remind myself to do every day. After all, this was God's command to Moses when the Lord parted the waters of the sea!"

Their train trip West was a long one. Each day, Miss Annie would answer more of Anna's questions about WMU. Anna learned about the children's groups. The youngest ones, the Sunbeams, studied about children in other lands. All the children brought their pennies and put them together so little children far across the world could hear how God loved them. Older children were called GAs, for Girl's Auxiliary and RAs (Royal Ambassadors) for the boys. Young adult women were Young Woman's Auxiliary. Each group had the same purpose: to share the message of God's love.

Anna wistfully commented, "Miss Annie, I wish I could have been one of those girls when I was young so I could have been part of helping children everywhere. However," she nodded her head and smiled, "I'm just an *old* GA at heart and can share God's message now and have experiences like riding on the range and visiting in tepees!"

The two ladies' first visit on this trip was to a frontier preacher's family. Annie was particularly excited about this visit. Back in 1890, she first learned about the dire needs of the frontier preachers and their families. WMU women began a special yearly project: sending frontier boxes. Sometimes these boxes were the only thing that made it possible for the frontier families to stay out West and preach.

Arriving in Blackwell, in Native American Territory, the two travelers found that the preacher was away on his "circuit," preaching in one little community after another. Mary, the preacher's wife, apologized, "My husband is so sorry to miss you. He is away a lot because these little towns are so scattered. He goes from one town to another, preaching. There are no full-time churches."

Annie and Mrs. Schimp smiled as each child in the little home shyly shook their hands. Annie knew how small the salaries were. The family only got about $200 a year, and half of that went for rent. The frontier boxes sent by WMU were essential for the family. The children looked forward with great anticipation to the arrival of the boxes. It was like Christmas. Thirteen-year-old Rebecca shyly smiled and said, "You know, the women who pack those boxes, they send such pretty clothes. It's like they were just made for me!" Miss Annie assured her, "They *are* made for you, and for each of the other children. Our women always put special treats and clothes in their boxes." At that remark, all the younger ones chimed in, "We like the candy in the boxes!" Upon hearing this, Annie silently gave thanks again for the wonderful boxes WMU women lovingly packed. Those boxes made a big difference.

Their next stop was the Kiowa reservation. Wearing her usual black dress with the beautiful cameo brooch at her neck, Annie Armstrong sat crisscross on the ground with the women and talked with them about the "Jesus Way." She ate their fatty stews and listened to their questions and prayed for each of them. She and Anna traveled next to Pawhuska, and from there, on to the nearby rolling prairies of the Osage reservation.

Their first meeting was outside. A group of Kiowa Christians had traveled many miles to share their faith. They explained to their Osage brothers that the Jesus road was good for the red man. Annie noticed that one tall man was standing apart from the other braves who were wrapped in their blankets and seated on the ground. She quietly asked him, "Can you understand about the Jesus way?" He looked at her, a question written on his face, and simply said, "I can, if you will tell it to me." Annie Armstrong told him the story of Jesus. Right then and there the two of them knelt together to pray to the God for whom he had been searching.

As Annie and Mrs. Schimp sat on the train headed East a few days later, Annie reflected on the wonderful trip and her highest moment of joy — the encounter with the man on the reservation who was now a fellow believer. One afternoon as the two women were chatting, Annie gave a gentle smile and remarked, "You know, we have had so many rich experiences. But I must say," and she nodded her head at the memory, "nothing felt more wonderful than to see that quiet, solemn Osage brave come to trust Jesus. It would have been worth these two thousand miles of travel just for that one moment."

THE REST OF THE STORY

Annie Armstrong would have been an outstanding head of whatever business was fortunate enough to have her leadership. Baptists can be eternally grateful that God led her to be the first executive leader of Woman's Missionary Union. She was wonderfully equipped. Annie was creative and full of ideas. She never did anything halfway. It was always with all her might and strength and skill. Above all, Annie was committed to be what God wanted her to be. She served him with all her heart, and she refused to take a salary. God also gave her a strong woman at her side. Sister Alice was friend, mentor, writer, and sounding board for her younger sibling.

Not only was Annie's *name* strong, her leadership and spirit were as well. She was not someone to be ignored. Annie worked in great harmony with the men who headed the major mission boards, both home and foreign. She also assisted and cooperated with the Sunday School Board. Those three board leaders knew they could count on Miss Annie to keep her word and do her job. Annie realized she had a quick temper, and often regretted things she said or wrote. One thing she did not do, however; she did not hold grudges.

Annie Armstrong literally worked day and night — often until far into the night. And Annie wrote letters! Long before there were computers, Annie Armstrong was typing and writing by hand thousands of letters. That was thousands of letters each *year*. Records show that one year alone, she wrote nearly 18,000 letters. Many nights, Annie went to bed late with her right hand cramped and hurting because she had written so much.

Annie was an organizational genius. She had the gift of getting different leaders to cooperate with other leaders who might not agree with them. All Baptists lost a real friend and leader when Annie stepped down in 1906 after eighteen years as the leader who helped start and form the organization. It became the largest union of women in the world who were banded together to do missions. Annie herself suggested that the missions offering at Christmas be named for Lottie Moon. Baptists happily agreed, and now, over a hundred years later, the offering still continues to grow.

When Annie retired as director, she indeed stepped down. She was not active in leadership from that point on. However, she did remain extremely active in missions work in Baltimore and through her church. And those Sunday School children continued to adore Miss Annie, the woman who loved them so much. She taught the children in her church for fifty years. When Annie was a stately eighty-three years old, Baptist women wanted to honor their first leader in a special way; they named the home mission offering (now North American) the Annie Armstrong Easter Offering. It has flourished, and Annie is remembered and honored each spring as boys, girls, men, and women give to the offering named for her.

Annie lived to be eighty-eight years old. In her final days, some of her WMU friends asked if she had any last words for all the dear women who loved missions. Annie gave a faint smile and her eyes crinkled as she answered, "Tell them to — Go Forward!"

Annie Armstrong at her Baltimore desk.

The Baltimore house where Annie Armstrong lived with her mother and sister Alice.

Portrait of Fannie Exile Heck

Chapter Seven

Fannie Finds a Way

"Mattie, my dear," Jonathan Heck spoke softly to his young wife as she sat rocking their fretful toddler. Little Fannie was flushed with a fever that persisted in spite of Mattie bathing her in cool water. Mattie looked into the eyes of her worried husband as Jonathan knelt beside her. He passed a soothing hand over Fannie's brow as he reminded his wife, "The war news is growing more frightening every day." Mattie nodded, seeming to catch a bit of the chill of fear that gripped her husband's heart.

Jonathan shook his head as he added, "Ever since General Sherman's march to the sea was completed last year, we've all known it was just a matter of time." He sighed, "You've seen them, Mattie, so many of our soldiers walking through the city, heading home ahead of the enemy. In no time, General Lee will have to surrender." Jonathan reached out and gripped her hand, "Mattie, Raleigh is right in the path of the advancing Union troops. I think we need to leave immediately and come back when things calm down."

Mattie looked deeply into his eyes, "But, Jonathan, Fannie is so feverish. Must we go now?" Then some of his urgency infected her, and she sat up straight and spoke resolutely, "We *will* go. You know best, and we must protect our little girls." Big sister Loula was nearly five and Fannie not quite three. Baby Minnie wasn't even a year old. Mattie rose at once and began gathering emergency supplies and food to take in their wagon. Two young teenaged boys on horseback agreed to accompany them in order to keep an eye out for danger and approaching soldiers.

About three o'clock the following afternoon, the two boys rode back to where the family in their wagon were slowly making their way along the road toward Fayetteville and comparative safety. "Soldiers are coming!" they cried out. "Union soldiers … coming down the road. Lots of them!"

Quickly, the frightened parents drove the wagon as best they could into the surrounding woods, out of sight of the marauding soldiers. Jonathan took one of the horses and rode ahead to try to spy out the danger so he could protect his wife and little ones. The hours dragged by before his return. Mattie had the sole responsibility over three helpless little girls, one of them burning with fever and one just a babe in arms. Memories of the agony in her heart while waiting hours in the dark woods remained with her for the rest of her life.

Jonathan returned late that night. Just before dawn, the Hecks cautiously made their way back to the road heading to Fayetteville and refuge. As daylight broke, Mattie's eyes went wide with astonishment at the desolation lying all around them. Houses had been burned, farms destroyed, and the whole area seemed deserted. Just as the tired young family reached Fayetteville and temporary safety, they heard the awful news. President Lincoln had been assassinated. Fresh fear struck their hearts, for such news could only mean more chaos in a country already torn apart by civil war.

As if to prove that bad *could* get worse, Fannie and baby Minnie both broke out with measles. The exposure from traveling through the countryside at night caused three-year-old Fannie's fever to turn into typhoid pneumonia. The young couple finally found a doctor, but he offered little hope. The parents wept as they gazed at little Fannie, lying limp in her father's arms. Mattie and Jonathan prayed as they had never before prayed. God answered their pleas. The fever left. For two weeks they watched at Fannie's bedside and nursed her slowly back to strength.

Soon able to return to Raleigh, the little family began the process of beginning life again in a nation torn apart by war. Jonathan, Fannie's father, had to travel a lot to rebuild his business. Her mother, Mattie, still only twenty-two, showed her grit and inner courage as she and the little ones recovered and gained strength. The First Baptist Church of Raleigh became their church home. Its people loved the Heck family and their growing brood of children.

Jonathan Heck was a keen businessman, and he prospered in business. He also enjoyed spending time with his family. He and his daughter Fannie were especially close. Fannie learned how to help her mother in the house, but she loved to go horseback riding with Papa. He taught her how to carefully shoot a gun, and she became a crack shot. Mattie's parents, the Callendines, soon came from West Virginia to live with them. Fannie and Grandmother Anna Callendine became especially close. Fannie would sit for hours and listen to Grandmama tell exciting stories of growing up. The bright young girl loved all the intriguing family tales dating back to the days of the Revolution, when America became an independent nation.

Fannie was an observant little girl. Several of her sisters were very outgoing and lively, but Fannie was the one who liked to "think long thoughts." She enjoyed sitting and listening to Papa and Mama talk "business" long into the evening. Fannie's father entrusted her mother with the planning and building of their home. (That house is still in Raleigh to this day, restored and beautiful like it was in the late 1860s.) The children loved to climb its spiral stairs up to the round tower above the third floor and look out at all of Raleigh spread below them.

The little Heck family became a larger family, as still more daughters and sons were born. Fannie had five sisters and four brothers who lived to adulthood. As next to the oldest, Fannie quickly learned how to care for the little ones. Each morning before breakfast, the family had devotions together. Papa read a passage from the Bible, and then everyone knelt and asked God to guide their day. These moments became a treasure in Fannie's memory and helped her as just a young child to depend on God.

Grandmama Callendine was a great influence in Fannie's life. When Fannie was nine, she and Grandmama read together each evening the biography of Ann Judson, America's first woman missionary. Ann was a real heroine of the past century. Fannie's eyes glowed as they read of Ann's adventures, her joys and fears and achievements. Sometimes Fannie would laugh at a story; other times, she would weep as she learned how Ann had suffered, all for the cause of sharing God's love. "Grandmama," she sometimes asked Anna, "do you think someday God could use *me* like that?" Anna Callendine gently smiled and patted Fannie's young hand, "My dear child, I have no doubt that God has special plans in mind for you. You just have a willing heart, and the dear Lord will lead you."

Young Fannie was painfully shy and disliked that in herself. She was determined to do something about it, so she worked at focusing on *others* and what she might do to help them. (In fact, Fannie became so skilled at focusing on others, it helped her forget about herself. She used that skill every day in future years when she became a national leader of women.) Fannie was also an avid reader and possessed an unusually retentive mind. At the same time, she became a keen judge of character.

The Heck home entertained many guests, especially those connected with Baptist work. Fannie met any number of Baptist church leaders and gained inspiration from many of them. Nine-year-old Fannie loved to listen to their stories. Dr. Taylor, the first president of the Foreign Mission Board, was one whose stories attracted her attention. Dr. Taylor had actually met Adoniram Judson himself way back in 1846. Fannie's eyes sparkled with excitement as she asked him to tell her about the great missionary. Dr. Taylor was amazed that so young a child knew the Judsons' story and gladly told her personal stories about the heroic young missionaries to Burma.

Mattie Heck was a leader of the women's missionary society in their Raleigh church. When Dr. Taylor sadly died in 1871, Dr. Henry Tupper became the new president. He had met Mattie Heck several years earlier. When he was a guest in their home during a Baptist convention, Dr. Tupper talked with Fannie's mother about involving other women in mission service. Fannie was fourteen that year and listened attentively as the president of the Foreign Mission Board asked her very own mother to form a committee to establish new missionary societies for women all over North Carolina.

"Our strength, Mrs. Heck," Dr. Tupper explained to Mattie, "is in working together to send more missionaries and more money to the fields overseas. More than anything, we need to *pray* for our missionaries." He concluded, "We would like for you to head up this work and lead the women of North Carolina to become involved and committed to sending the gospel to the world." Mattie agreed, and during the next year, she and her committee were able to report to the state Baptist convention that there were now seventeen active missionary societies for women.

Teenaged Fannie was at the state Baptist meeting and was thrilled with the report. But suddenly, several older men spoke up, saying that women needed to stop such work. If they didn't, they would just want to take over and that wasn't women's work! Mattie Heck was devastated at the response; however, Fannie was inspired. She vowed that very day to do all she could to *help* women work for the Lord, just as God would want them to.

Fannie was already at college at Hollins in Virginia, and her favorite subject was elocution (the skill of speaking clearly.) All her brothers and sisters, as well as her parents, were amazed that shy, introverted Fannie excelled at speaking. (And God used that special skill to help her become a great leader of women.) One day Fannie was talking with one of the history professors, and learned that a well-known Hollins graduate was now a missionary in China. Fannie's heart skipped a beat when the professor revealed that none other than Lottie Moon herself had been a student at Hollins. Miss Moon seemed more real and personal to Fannie when she learned that Lottie had been a teenager at Hollins just like herself.

Fannie's younger brothers and sisters loved summertime when their adored sister was home. Nobody could tell a story quite like Fannie. Jonathan Heck was now a leader in Baptist churches, both his own and in the state convention. He delighted in taking Fannie to state meetings and national convention meetings as well. Always an attentive listener, Fannie absorbed what she heard and what her eyes observed.

When she was about twenty, Fannie finally met a young businessman who lived up to the standards she thought important in a man. She had about despaired of ever meeting someone who measured up to her ideal, someone like her father. But her young friend contracted tuberculosis and in less than two years, lost his hold on life. Fannie was devastated, her heart crushed. Over a period of months and years, she reconciled herself to the reality of what had happened. She did not become bitter, but never again did Fannie show an interest in anyone else.

God had an interest in *her,* however, and that soon became apparent. She wholeheartedly put her faith in Christ. Within months, Fannie was asked to teach a class of teenaged boys. She taught that class many years and influenced countless young men who never forgot the truths Fannie Heck taught them. Together, she and her friend Sally Bailey began a project to help young Raleigh girls who were growing up in poverty. At a nearby church, the two young women taught the girls how to sew, how to prepare to earn a livelihood, and how Christ could make a difference in their hearts. Helping others was exhilarating and made Fannie even more determined to pass on the blessings God had showered on her.

Fannie, with her lustrous brown eyes and shining curls, was someone people remembered after meeting her. She had a *presence*. God had gifted her with the ability to make those around her feel important and needed. Fannie became extremely active in her church's women's missionary society and worked alongside her own mother and Annie Skinner, their pastor's wife. Fannie's leadership and enthusiasm infected the other women of the society, all older than she. Age didn't seem to matter. Twenty-three-year-old Fannie Heck was already a respected leader.

That fall, Fannie went with her father to the state Baptist convention. Her father was state Sunday School superintendent, and she beamed with pride as he gave his report. The highlight of the convention for Fannie was the testimony of two young missionary couples going overseas for the first time. Both from North Carolina, David and Maggi Herring, and Dr. R.T. Bryan and Lulu, were going to China. Fannie sat enthralled as they related their call to service. Yet again did her own heart wonder how God might use her. Wistfully, she thought, *Oh God, I wish I could go to China as a missionary too.* She so much wanted to be what *He* wanted her to be.

Baptist leaders recognized something of the talents of this impressive young woman. Within two months, God's call would come knocking at the door of the Heck home. Fannie recalled how

Grandmama Callendine had repeatedly assured her, "God has His place for you, Fannie. He will reveal it to you." Dr. Theodore Whitfield was a well-known Baptist pastor and leader in North Carolina. He was also the North Carolina vice president of the Foreign Mission Board. He came to their home with a request of Miss Heck.

The distinguished pastor cleared his throat and said, "Miss Heck, the Foreign Mission Board has a proposal to set before you." It was a moment Fannie would remember the rest of her life. There was a feeling of destiny about it. Ringing in her ears were the words Grandmama Callendine had spoken just weeks earlier, "Fannie, I do not doubt that God is going to open a way for you, a special way."

Dr. Whitfield explained that the board wanted her to head up "a central committee" to organize mission societies all over North Carolina. Fannie's mind buzzed with memories. This was what her own mama had wanted to do ten years earlier and men would not allow it. *This time,* she silently vowed, *Baptist leaders are ready, and so are we women!* She agreed to be president of the committee, and her own dear friend Sallie would be secretary. Fannie's mind was humming with ideas and plans. A team of sixteen women, with their two leaders the youngest of the group, became a powerhouse of missions excitement.

Fannie began contacting and planning. Her own mama's dreams some ten years before were now becoming reality. North Carolina women had no set missions program, no plan of how to begin the work. Fannie and Sallie learned by doing. Fannie started a newsletter, *Missionary Talk,* that would provide information and stories for groups of women and children to use. Fannie had help from several of her brothers and sisters with wrapping and mailing material and stuffing envelopes. Sometimes the Heck parlor was a beehive of noise and happy activity as eager young hands helped out. Even her nine-year-old brother, John, was a willing worker.

Fannie wrote to women leaders in other states and shared ideas, learning what those women had found successful. Amazingly, that very first year, seventy-four new women's societies were formed in North Carolina. Fannie knew without a doubt that it was God at work. In addition, all across the nation, Baptist women who loved missions were informally meeting together each year when the Southern Baptist Convention met. Fannie happily attended those meetings.

There was a new feeling of excitement among those women. They were talking seriously about *really* organizing, just like Methodist and Presbyterian women had been doing for several years. Fannie learned that Lottie Moon had been writing a lot of letters to Miss Annie Armstrong from Maryland and to several other strong leaders as well. Lottie explained that those other women's groups were already at work supporting missionaries in China and other countries. They were strong, Miss Moon explained, because they worked together. Fannie recognized a strong leader in Miss Armstrong when she talked about Miss Moon and her ideas. Annie urged the women to do as Lottie recommended and become a real team.

When 1888 arrived, Mattie Heck was asked to preside at the women's meeting that was to be held while the Southern Baptist Convention was meeting in Richmond, Virginia. Mattie had to regretfully turn down the invitation. She was expecting yet another baby at age forty-five and her health was precarious. However, Fannie attended the meeting and listened with glowing eyes to the speeches and reports from the many states. She was the youngest delegate there, but Fannie was as excited as any of them when on May 14, Woman's Missionary Union, Auxiliary of the Southern Baptist Convention, was officially organized.

WMU blossomed and grew — and no one was more active and involved than Fannie Heck. She worked ceaselessly to promote the work of the Sunbeams, teaching little children about the needs of the world. There were some older youth groups known as Young Women's Auxiliary, but no organization for girls or for boys who were nine to sixteen. Fannie felt that such groups were extremely important and began thinking about how to bring them about. She admired the leadership of Miss Annie Armstrong, that tall, stately woman who liked to wear black and always had a beautiful cameo brooch at her throat. Fannie felt like Miss Armstrong not only acted like a wise leader but *looked* like one as well. Miss Martha McIntosh, the new WMU president, was short, slender and quiet, but she too revealed a keen and kind mind and real leadership ability.

In 1892, Miss McIntosh quietly told Annie Armstrong that she would not be able to serve as president the following year. Annie asked her, "Do you have in mind someone you think might be an effective leader?" Mattie McIntosh's blue eyes twinkled. "I do indeed. I feel like Miss Fannie Heck has shown herself to have fine leadership qualities." Miss McIntosh emphasized, "I know she's young — but she is oh so capable!"

The following May 1892, when Mattie McIntosh regretfully announced she would be unable to serve again, the women turned immediately to Fannie Heck. She was unanimously elected. At twenty-nine, she became the youngest woman in all WMU history to ever serve as national WMU president. At her election in 1892, Fannie Heck had a moment she would treasure the rest of her life. The renowned missionary from China, Lottie Moon herself, was actually on furlough and attended the meeting where Fannie was elected. Fannie was in awe as she had the privilege of meeting that remarkable woman who had given her life in service to the people of China.

At the annual meeting the following year, in Nashville, Lottie Moon was once again with them. She was soon to return to China, and this was Lottie's opportunity to encourage and uplift the women who supported her. Fannie was honored to present Miss Moon to the delegates. She smiled to herself as she saw together on the platform the stately six-foot-tall Annie Armstrong standing next to her treasured friend, Lottie Moon, all four-feet-some-seven-inches of her. Lottie Moon spoke of God at work in China, and women were thrilled to listen to the testimony of such a remarkable woman. Lottie Moon herself led a dedicatory prayer to conclude the meeting. Fannie felt like her cup of joy was overflowing.

In her heart that day Fannie vowed, *Oh God, help me endeavor to see the needs of the world from Your standpoint. Help me plan not for the year, but for the years.* God honored that prayer of His faithful servant, Fannie Heck. For many years to come, He used Fannie to touch and impact countless lives.

THE REST OF THE STORY

Fannie Heck was not only the youngest ever president of Woman's Missionary Union. She was also the longest-serving. Miss Heck was president three different times, for a total of fifteen years. Fannie's last fourteen months were spent in constant pain in a cancer hospital, but she continued to lead through letters and by meeting with women leaders like Kathleen Mallory, who came to Fannie's bedside. Miss Mallory was also quite young. She was the national director for the last three years of Fannie's life. Every day without fail, Kathleen wrote a letter or card to her beloved Miss Heck.

Fannie became the most quoted woman ever in Southern Baptist history. Because of Fannie's keen leadership, Royal Ambassadors was born, as was Girl's Auxiliary for girls too old for Sunbeams but too young for Young Woman's Auxiliary.

WMU women often referred to Fannie Heck as the most accomplished and capable woman in Southern Baptist life. Over 100 years after her death, Fannie Heck is still quoted. Her ideas and dreams for WMU and missions live on. She began the first WMU magazine, the first prayer calendar, and the children's organizations, both RAs and GAs. Hers was the creative genius behind what has come to be known as Mission Action. Fannie was the guiding light in the organizations for children and youth in missions. Among her greatest gifts were wisdom and vision. Fannie beautifully "planned for the years" and left that gift to all of us, both young and old. She had a remarkable ability to "think long thoughts" and look to the future. Fannie Heck loved to tell children, "Remember, those who bring sunshine into the lives of others cannot keep it from themselves."

Let's go bring that sunshine!

Fannie on porch of Heck House, Raleigh, North Carolina, with her mother Mattie and brother Charlie and wife.

Kathleen Mallory at 33

Chapter Eight

Kathleen Mallory: The Tiny Dynamo

Kathleen, her bright blue eyes looking unusually serious, spoke up as soon as Hugh Mallory finished reading a passage from Matthew at family devotions time. "Father," she quietly announced, "I am going to join the church at the next service." Her voice had a tone of determination threaded through it. Her parents exchanged a quick glance, and Hugh cleared his throat, "My child, this is a most important decision, and it must not be made in haste." Kathleen's bright young face became very sober. She brushed back a curl and turned to her mother, Louisa, her eyes asking a question. Louisa gently spoke, "Kathleen, let's talk it over when you come in from school."

That evening, mother and daughter had a long talk. Louisa quickly realized that Kathleen knew her own heart and understood the decision she was making. The next evening, Kathleen met with their pastor, Dr. James Frost. He listened intently as the tiny young girl, who looked about six or seven but sounded like a young woman twice that age, answered each probing question he asked. He realized at once that here was a child who had trusted Christ and wanted to share that news with her church family.

The following Sunday morning, Kathleen was ready for church ahead of everyone in the family, including her five brothers and sisters. As the invitation was given at the conclusion of the service, Kathleen walked calmly down the aisle to profess her faith in Christ. It was a day never to be forgotten. Kathleen was so petite that Dr. Frost had to carry her in his arms into the baptismal pool. From that day on, there was a new sense of purpose about young Kathleen.

The Mallorys lived in Selma, a beautiful little town in south Alabama. Like most other places in the South, Selma was working hard to recover from the destruction caused by the Civil War. Kathleen's father was a leading lawyer in the town, as well as a prominent Baptist layman (volunteer worker in the church) in Alabama. Kathleen's mother was a wise and tender woman, brilliant of mind and tender of heart. Louisa faithfully taught her youngsters the importance of putting others before themselves and to always listen to the ideas of others. Kathleen didn't realize how much she was like Louisa. Even their speech patterns were similar. Most of the time, Louisa inverted her sentences, never starting one with "I." Her young daughter developed a similar way of speech, like saying, "Happy am I that it was a special day at school today," or "Excited I am to be able to go with you, Father." This unusual way of speaking became a lifelong habit.

Kathleen was small of frame, but she possessed a giant and retentive mind. Some of her friends fussed about attending school, but Kathleen loved the daily challenge. Of all the rigorous coursework at Dallas Academy, where the Mallory children went to school, Latin was Kathleen's favorite. Louisa Mallory understood her six children very well and occasionally commented on their character traits. She acknowledged Kathleen's engaging and sweet nature as well as her strong sense of determination. Louisa often commented, "Why, anyone can get along with Kathleen as long as they do things her way!"

Something else her mother noticed about Kathleen was her incredible self-discipline. Even as a little tyke, she would stay at a task until it was completed. (The grown-up Kathleen did the same thing, and it was one of the reasons for her remarkable success as a leader.) She eagerly looked forward to college and to learning all she could. Kathleen had tempting offers from the largest universities in Alabama, but to her parents' surprise, she wanted to attend Goucher College for women in Baltimore, Maryland. Her parents were a bit puzzled at her determination but allowed her to make her own choice.

Eighteen-year-old Kathleen stepped off the train in Baltimore into a whole new world. She was on her own and excited about it. Here she was, a young woman from a small town in Alabama, becoming part of a major city of more than half a million people. Kathleen, with her deep faith and brilliant mind, was up to the challenge. She made friends so quickly within the first month that she was elected president of the freshman class. One of her closest friends was May Keller. May was from Baltimore but lived in the dorm at Goucher. She and Kathleen took the streetcar each Sunday to Eutaw Place Baptist Church. There, Kathleen met the well-known leader of Woman's Missionary Union, Miss Annie Armstrong. She greatly admired that remarkable woman.

On a weekend visit to May Keller's home, Kathleen met Janney Lupton. May's mother had invited several guests to a party for May and her college friends. One of the guests was a young intern from Johns Hopkins Medical School. Janney was a handsome young man with black hair and a winsome smile. Immediately, Kathleen was taken with his sparkling brown eyes and engaging grin. In turn, Janney was captivated by the petite young student with the lovely Southern accent and intensely blue eyes. It was the beginning of a love story.

Within the year, Kathleen and Janney knew they were in love and wished to spend the rest of their lives together. Both were intent and determined and willing to wait until Kathleen finished school and Janney could do his internship and residency. They planned that he would set up his practice, and then they would marry. Their feet were on the ground, but sometimes Kathleen felt like she was floating around with her head in the clouds. Love was wonderful.

The sweethearts visited each other when they could, and letters flew back and forth. Each of them looked eagerly to the day they could speak their wedding vows and begin "living happily ever after." Then one day, a letter came that caused Kathleen's beautiful blue eyes to fill with tears and her heart skip a beat in fear. Janney had just been diagnosed with the dread disease of tuberculosis. How could it have happened? Janney played down its danger and spoke of treatment and recovery, but Kathleen feared the worst. After months in a sanitorium, Janney was finally declared free of disease and his fiancée's face lighted up with joy. That wonderful Christmas, Kathleen and Janney happily planned for their summer wedding in Selma.

Then came February. Janney was called on a bitterly cold night to deliver a baby in a nearby village in the mountains. Caught in a freezing rainstorm, he contracted a nasty cold. For two weeks, Kathleen anxiously waited for a letter. Nothing. She knew something must be amiss. Janney usually wrote every day. Sure enough, the next morning, Mrs. Lupton sent a telegram. "Come at once. Janney is ill." Ever afterwards, Kathleen recalled the sharp living pain of anguish that ripped at her heart through each long hour of every day that last month of Janney's life. She sat day after day at the bedside of her beloved, and a little piece of her heart seemed to wither away bit by bit. One chilly morning the last week of March, Janney slipped into eternity. Kathleen felt like an essential part of herself was forever gone. How could she bear the pain?

Her emotions did not show on the outside. Kathleen was too private for that. But long into the night, one after another, she lay sleepless while silent tears trickled onto her pillow. *Why? Why? Why?* There was never an answer. Her parents felt helpless. They did not want to intrude on her sorrow, but they were worried about her stoic quietness. Kathleen spent many hours reading, especially Scripture. It comforted her heart, but she knew she needed purpose. Surely God had something in mind for her life. Well-meaning friends suggested she teach school. She had already tried that one year and immediately laughed and said, "Oh, no. I'm too bossy to teach!"

Kathleen's parents longed for her to have a purpose again and prayed about how they might help. Hugh Mallory was president of the Alabama Baptist Convention that year, and he had an idea. A letter had come from their missionary in North China who worked with the legendary Miss Lottie Moon. Hugh asked his daughter to read that letter to the women of the state. They would be at their annual WMU meeting in the town of Roanoke at the same time as the state Baptist convention. Kathleen graciously agreed to share the letter with the ladies. Little did she know that while reading the letter to the women of WMU, God would speak directly to her *own* heart.

The second morning of the state meeting, Kathleen went to the platform to read the letter from Anna Hartwell that told of the crying needs in work Anna shared with Miss Moon. Suddenly, it was as if Kathleen's own eyes were opened, and she could literally *see* those pleading souls in faraway China. It was as if the letter was speaking straight to her own heart, and she knew she wanted to spend the rest of her life serving God. It was at that meeting that the women of Alabama fell in love with the beautiful young woman from Selma who captivated their hearts.

Changes seemed to come rapidly. Kathleen was asked to be volunteer leader for Alabama Young Women's Auxiliary. She accepted the new challenge and went to work with a will, traveling to many churches across the state to encourage groups of young ladies and to help new groups organize. The girls loved the beautiful young leader and responded quickly to her leadership. In fact, by the next state meeting, women across Alabama recognized her keen abilities of leadership, and she was asked to be the leader of Alabama WMU. Kathleen was shocked at the invitation. And yet, she felt a sense of inevitability. Had she not been praying that God would show her His will for her life? At that same meeting, Edith Crane, who was national WMU director, was present and recognized the talents of young Miss Mallory. She saw in her real possibilities for the future.

Kathleen, with her usual incredible discipline of time and skills, went right to work in her new office in Montgomery, the state capital. She worked at her desk from early morning until late at night unless she was on the road. She traveled a lot, speaking and encouraging women's groups all over the state. Soon Kathleen Mallory became known as "a fine little businesswoman." She looked dainty and gentle, but she could work circles around many of the Baptist men in leadership. They secretly nicknamed her the "Tiny Dynamo." And in just months, she was given another nickname, "the sweetheart of Alabama," because of her winsome personality and love for others.

Kathleen was stunned the morning she opened a letter from Miss Fannie Heck, the national president of Woman's Missionary Union. She read that Edith Crane was resigning as national director because of illness. Would Miss Mallory consent to have her name placed in nomination? Kathleen's head began to buzz. *Me? National director? Surely not! I am only 33. I have so little experience.* Then, as Kathleen always did when faced with a huge question, she sank to her knees in prayer. Writing her parents to seek their advice, she soon received a letter from her father. "Kathleen," he wrote, "if duty calls, it must be answered. I wish you to do what our Master would have you do." With trembling hands and heart, Kathleen replied to the letter, saying she would consider the position.

The bright May morning in Oklahoma City, when more than a thousand women gathered for their annual meeting, was an occasion forever etched in Kathleen's mind. When her name was placed in nomination, Miss Heck asked her to come to the platform. As Kathleen made her way to the stage, one longtime leader in WMU leaned over to whisper to her neighbor, "There's just one thing I don't like about her." Surprised, her friend frowned and asked, "What is *that?*" The matron smiled and replied. "She's so young!" As soon as Kathleen was elected, she was asked to speak. In her rich, slow voice, Kathleen looked earnestly at the large audience and said, "Let us pray." She immediately fell to her knees there on the platform and poured out her heart to God; it was just as if she was speaking to her beloved father.

And through thirty-six rich years of service, Kathleen Mallory prayed on her knees and thousands of women joined her, humbling themselves before God. The "Tiny Dynamo" went to work, both day and night. She was the first at the office in the morning, and the last to leave at night. She and Fannie Heck were an amazing team, working together for three years. Tragically, Fannie discovered she had incurable cancer. For fourteen months she lay in a women's hospital in Richmond, Virginia. Never a day was she without pain. Fannie Heck led from her bed and, remarkably, never complained. And every day, for all fourteen months, Kathleen wrote her a note or a letter.

Along with all the duties of WMU's leader, Kathleen became editor of their magazine. She traveled thousands of miles, often by train. To save time, she would work on her editing and writing responsibilities while spending hours on trains. She was especially happy in 1938 when the Christmas offering for foreign missions was named for their beloved Lottie Moon.

Miss Mallory's thirty-six years in office had its share of crises — from World War I to the Great Depression and on through World War

II. Kathleen often told audiences when she spoke, "There are three things we women hate: the Devil, Dirt, and Debt!" With Kathleen leading, an amazing thing happened. Although women in the 1930s very seldom worked outside the home, it was WMU offerings that saved the mission boards. Right in the heart of the Great Depression, unemployment in America reached a staggering 25 percent. WMU became responsible for guaranteeing the support of 100 missionaries through the Lottie Moon offering. In that one year alone, a massive 70 percent of the Foreign Mission Board's income came from WMU offerings. Without WMU, both foreign and home mission boards would not have survived and our missionaries would have had to return home.

The remarkable Kathleen Mallory lived a remarkably simple life. She never owned a car. She never owned a house. The WMU headquarters building was in Birmingham, Alabama, and Kathleen lived in an efficiency apartment. Two of her nieces visited "Artie," as they called their favorite aunt one summer afternoon. Looking around the tiny apartment, one of the girls looked puzzled and asked, "Artie, where is your *bed?*" Kathleen gave her little grin and said, "Watch." Walking over to the wall, she pulled the Murphy bed down from its hiding spot in the wall itself. Their beloved aunt had a tiny kitchen with a small refrigerator and one electric burner for a stove. "How do you cook meals on one eye?" the girls asked. Kathleen smiled happily and said, "I don't cook much, you see. At night, I usually eat part of a can of spinach and a boiled egg. But I like ice cream," she added. "I have an ice cream treat quite often!"

Thirty-six years of leadership left Kathleen richly satisfied with God's calling on her life. It also left her weary and recognizing it was time to retire. A beautiful and dynamic young leader was chosen to step into her position, and Kathleen was thrilled with her successor, Alma Hunt. WMU was in good hands. On her last night of service, Kathleen Mallory stayed in her office long after the building was empty of staff.

She wrote a note for Alma and left it on the desk for her to find the next morning. She then walked to the entrance of the building, stood and looked around the large area. Kathleen gave a smile, half sad and half joyful, and opened the door to leave. It seemed as if she could hear the whisper from the Master, *Well done, my good and faithful servant.*

The Rest of the Story

Kathleen eventually returned to her beloved hometown of Selma and spent the last years of her life in a new apartment structure that was built right next to her home church. Each morning she awoke to the sight, right outside her window, of the magnificent steeple of First Baptist Church. All sorts of nieces and nephews lived in Selma and loved to visit with their treasured "Artie." She had more invitations to go out to eat than she had time to go to them.

Kathleen Mallory was rich in beautiful memories. Her nephew Edgar was a prominent lawyer in Selma. He loved to spoil "Artie," and they would often chuckle over long-ago happenings. "I remember one time," Edgar told her, "my folks were away and I was committed to your special care." Interested in his memory, Kathleen replied, "Yes?" Edgar smiled, "Artie, you made me wash my feet *every* day and … ." She couldn't stop her chuckle, "Edgar, you were a dirty little boy." He smiled and continued, "Yes, but you made me wash my feet every time *before* I got in the tub!"

Alabama's day of prayer for state missions was named the Mallory Offering in honor of Kathleen. in 1954, that day fell on June 17. And that was the day Kathleen met her Savior face to face. In the last moments, a look of beautiful peace crept across her face. It could have been that, in those very moments, there came to her mind's eye the glorified faces of her mother and her father. And there also, ever young, ever smiling, the beloved face of her Janney. Above all else, Kathleen Mallory saw her Savior, face to face.

*Kathleen at three,
Selma, Alabama*

*Kathleen Mallory
at Goucher College,
Baltimore, Maryland*

*Dr. Janney Lupton, the
love of Kathleen's life*

*Kathleen Mallory
at her desk in Baltimore*

Gladys Aylward with Alice and Jody Hunt
New Year's Day 1964 — Taipei, Taiwan

Chapter Nine

Gladys Aylward: Small Woman, Giant Heart

A frightened young Gladys Aylward stood before the middle school headmaster. Her knees were trembling so badly that she was afraid he could see them shaking. Gladys wracked her brain to think of why she had been summoned: *I try so hard. I never make trouble. What have I done?* The headmaster looked down at the records in his hand, then up at the small fourteen-year-old standing nervously before him. Her big brown eyes full of questions, Gladys spoke "Sir, you wanted to see me?"

Clearing his throat, the headmaster answered, "Gladys, I'm sorry, but you will need to leave school." Gladys was stunned. *Leave?* He continued, "I see that you have not passed a single examination since you entered middle school." Again, he cleared his throat and concluded, "I'm sorry." Gladys' ears buzzed with shock. What would happen to her? What could she do? She gulped, "Yes sir." Gladys slowly turned and walked out the door, closing behind her the path to an education. Teeth clenched tightly together, she fought back tears as she plodded home. Mum, in her matter-of-fact way, put a cup of tea in front of Gladys and talked to her daughter about what to do next. Father soon trudged home from his job delivering mail and patted her back, gruffly saying,

"Never mind, Gladys. We'll work something out."

The Aylwards' London suburb of Edmonton was full of working-class people like their own family. Everyone was simply trying day by day to make a living. Nonetheless, Gladys realized there was something a bit different about her family. They loved God. Mum and Father took their four children to church every Sunday. Each of them had asked Christ to come into their hearts. Gladys was unlike many of her friends. She never doubted God. If God promised something, her simple faith told her that He would do it. Just now, however, she was crushed with disappointment. She felt like a failure. But Gladys drew a deep breath and reminded herself, *God hasn't changed. He will take care of me, even if I am not clever.*

It was 1916 and everyone in England was uneasy. World War I engulfed the whole world. Gladys, her sister, and their two brothers quickly learned to head for the bomb shelter when the sirens warned of approaching German planes. Fear was a common part of nearly every day. Young Gladys soon found a job as a parlor maid. She might not be clever at books and math and science, but she excelled at being practical. She soon learned the skills useful for a maid of all work. In her snowy white cap and apron, Gladys was a whiz at cleaning, dusting, and greeting guests. She could do any chore around the house. Had not Mum always taught her how to do her part?

Each day, Gladys did her work promptly and looked at life with practical eyes. To the young parlor maid, black was black and white was white — no shades in between. She still did not like to read, but the Bible was more than a book to her. It was God speaking. She set herself to memorizing long passages of precious promises. Her church was very important, and she faithfully attended every week. Above all, she loved hymns and music. Many years later, Gladys recalled the bombing raids. When the sirens blew, all the neighbors raced to their nearby shelter, including the frightened children. Gladys went to the small pump organ that stood in the corner of the shelter and played rousing hymns. The young children gathered around, and everyone sang at the top of their lungs, drowning out the sound of incoming bombers.

Sometimes their small church had visiting preachers. One of those was a missionary who told about the millions of poor people in China who had never heard there was a living God who loved them. The thought caught her heart and imagination. She couldn't pass a test, but Gladys somehow *knew* that God wanted her to tell those people in China about him. As time passed, the conviction grew. She knew that she must go to China. When she told her friends, they thought she was "barmy," touched in the head. *Gladys Aylward? A parlor maid? A missionary in China?* Mum did not scoff at her, though; she simply said, "Gladys, if this is how God leads you, I stand in support." (And her mother did support her — over many years.)

By persevering, Gladys finally saved enough money to go to missionary training. Because of her poor school record, the principal of the theology school looked dubious. Finally, he decided to let her try for three months of the three-year study. They would see how she did. Three months later, she stood yet again in the dreaded spot before the school principal. She heard the same message fourteen-year-old Gladys had heard. "Miss Aylward, I am so sorry. In these three months you have not passed a single test. And even if you were to pass, the studies take three years to complete. By then you would be thirty." The principal concluded with a sad shake of his head, "And how could you ever learn a difficult foreign language at that age?"

The determination in her large dark eyes not wavering, Gladys responded, "Thank you anyway, sir. However, God wants me in China. So I will go." She walked out of the office, her steps firm, her heart still set on China. Her first stop that afternoon was a travel agency. "What does it cost to go to China?" she asked the agent. Rather startled, the man quoted a price. It sounded gigantic to Gladys' shocked ears. Wincing, she inquired, "Is there any *cheaper* way?" The man shook his head, then added, "Well, you can go overland by train, but it is a long and very dangerous trip." Even the price of the train ticket sounded huge to Gladys. She asked, "Can I pay a little along?" Very reluctantly the clerk agreed, and Gladys began saving money to go to China.

Gladys thought it over, asking herself, *What do I know how to do? I know how to be a good parlor maid.* She soon found a job and began saving. It took many months, but the wonderful day finally arrived. She had enough money to go to China. Gladys was tiny, only four-feet-ten, but she was nothing if not practical and determined. She gathered the bare essentials for the long journey. A tearful but loving Aylward family stood on the train platform waving and weeping as Gladys left London terminal, bound for faraway lands. The long and dangerous train journey would have daunted even a brave man. The trip seemed endless, but a determined and single-minded Gladys Aylward set her eyes on China. She knew she did not go alone. God was with her.

Many years later, Gladys told friends a bit about that harrowing journey. She was a small, lone, foreign woman, unable to speak the languages of the various countries through which the train passed. She was literally going to China on faith. Gladys left London with a two-pound traveler's check in her pocket and ninepence in change nestled next to the check. Only by God's protection did she escape being assaulted, robbed, or even killed during her endless train journey to China. The weeks traveling through Russia were very perilous. It was 1930, and much of the world was teetering on the brink of war. No place was safe. Miraculously, Gladys safely arrived in China a month later at the age of twenty-eight.

Before she left London, Gladys learned of an elderly missionary widow, Jeannie Lawson. Jeannie lived in far distant *Shan Si* (Shahn She) Province in Northwest China. Yangcheng, a little walled city in a valley between high, bare mountains, was her home. Mrs. Lawson was working alone and badly needed help. She was trying to redo a run-down old inn to be a usable hostel for muleteers. Many men traveled through the countryside delivering goods by mule. Jeannie hoped to house and feed them. Most importantly, she wanted to tell them stories from the Bible at night. Everyone loved a story.

Jeannie was old and tired, but her face lighted up when an exhausted Gladys Aylward arrived at her door. She introduced herself to a delighted Mrs. Lawson, who welcomed her with a broad sweep of her hand, "Come on in! Let's get to work." They became a team along with old *Yang* (Yahng), the cook. *Yang* (Yahng) had a deeply wrinkled mountaineer's face and a beaming smile. Behind that smile was a sharp mind and a tender heart. Gladys looked worried when Jeannie said they would soon be ready for customers. "But Mrs. Lawson, I can't speak a word of Chinese. I have no money to study the language."

Yang (Yahng) smiled even more broadly and pointed to himself, "Miss Gladys, your language teacher will be *Yang* (Yahng). Not to worry!" Astoundingly, Gladys Aylward, who could not pass a simple test at missionary training school, learned the difficult Chinese language quite quickly. She soon could speak like one of the locals in their little city of Yangcheng. Furthermore, she learned to both read and write Chinese characters.

The three of them got the inn ready, but they needed customers. Many people in the city were leery of foreigners. Children and adults alike called them *"Yang Gweidz"* (Yahng Gwaydz), or foreign devils. Gladys' first assignment at the inn was to get the leader of the mule train to stop at this new hostel named Inn of Six Happinesses. Gladys learned to call out, *"Mei You Chung Dz. Mei You Tao Dz. Hau Hau. Lai*

Lai." (May oh chong. May oh taw dz. Haw Haw, Lie Lie). Gladys laughed when she learned what the words meant: "We have no bugs, We have no fleas. Good. Good. Come. Come." Her job was to grab the lead mule by its halter and all the other mules would follow. To Gladys' amazement, it worked.

All too quickly, tragedy hit. Mrs. Lawson fell from a ladder and did not survive. Gladys was alone once more, this time in a strange land among strangers, barely able to speak the strange language. But in her heart, she never doubted she was where God wanted her to be. Night after night, she and *Yang* (Yahng) cooked and cared for animals and told stories from the Bible. The men all slept on the large *kang* (kahng), a bed of bricks that was heated underneath by pipes from the cooking stove. The special feature of this inn was storytelling, and word spread to muleteers near and far — *You can hear good stories for free at the new inn.*

Gladys had a big problem. The customers barely paid enough for her to buy food for them. What to do? Then, the Mandarin himself, the head official of the city of Yangcheng, made a surprise appearance at their inn. Old *Yang* (Yahng) was frightened, but the small foreign lady was made of sterner stuff. Gladys was polite and respectful. Nonetheless, she admitted to herself that she was a bit overwhelmed at the sight of the mighty Mandarin, in his beautiful red silk clothing, standing at her door.

Happily, Gladys soon discovered that she was not in trouble. Instead, the Mandarin wanted her to become the "official foot unbinder." For hundreds of years in China, the custom was to bind the feet of little girls so they would be a prize on the marriage market. Tiny feet were considered beautiful. Those same tiny feet were also terribly painful. Little girls would cry in agony as their mothers were forced to bind the cloth wrappings around their feet tighter and tighter every day, crushing the toes and foot together to make them little.

The Mandarin informed her that the new government was now outlawing bound feet. However, he needed help to enforce the new law. He explained, "Miss Aylward, I have come for your help." Gladys' face showed her shock, "My help?" she echoed. "Yes," he replied, "I have come about your feet." Now Gladys was really puzzled. "What?" The Mandarin gave a little smile, "I have come because you have big feet." Gladys looked down at her dainty size 3 feet and exclaimed, "Big? These are big?" Mandarin smiled and further explained, "A man cannot examine girls' feet. And *you* are the only woman in the area with unbound feet."

The Mandarin offered her a small salary and would send two soldiers with her to enforce the rules. Suddenly, she who had no money, not even enough to buy food for their customers, would now have a salary. Not only that, but she would be able to travel to all the villages around their city and tell the people about Jesus! In that very moment, Gladys gave thanks in her heart to God. He was providing for her an income *and* giving her a way to take the gospel to hundreds of people in many villages. And as the years passed, the little girls had their feet unbound and the pain gone. Furthermore, people in all the villages learned of a God who loved them. Small village churches were planted all over that region of China, and Gladys rejoiced.

She felt more Chinese than English by this time. She applied and was accepted for Chinese citizenship. Gladys realized that much of the time she even *thought* like a Chinese would. She felt at home and at peace, even hard as life was. She often thought, "The villagers' minds were bound by sin and superstition. But now, their minds are unbound, just like the little girls' feet. Now they have peace instead of pain."

Gladys was also given a wonderful Chinese name. Those who knew her began using this special name. *Ai Weh Deh* (Eye Way Duh) meant "the virtuous one — the good one" because the people saw her love for them and the way she helped them. The Mandarin came to rely on her and to trust her. Gladys was even called on to stop a riot in the prison. Remarkably, she calmed the prisoners down. After the riot, Gladys demanded that the prisoners' lives be made better. Gladys insisted, "Feed them properly and let them earn money." As a result, the poor, ragged prisoners were forever grateful to *Ai Weh Deh* (Eye Way Duh)

Greatly to her own surprise, Gladys soon became a mother to many. One day she saw a tiny scrap of a little girl being abused by a gypsy woman at the side of the road. The waif was almost dead of starvation. Gladys couldn't stand it. She asked for the child, and the evil woman finally sold the little one for all the money *Ai Weh Deh* (Eye Way Duh) had, ninepence (about fourteen cents). Gladys took the little one home. She cleaned and fed her. Soon the small girl looked like an entirely different child. The name Ninepence stuck, and forever after, that became her name. First one child was left at the inn, then another. Soon Gladys was caring for at least twenty children, ranging in age from toddlers to teenagers.

However, all too soon, life changed. War drew closer and closer. One quiet morning, the peace of Yangcheng was forever shattered. There was a strange humming sound, and people ran out of their houses and saw little silver planes shining in the sun. Everyone shouted and waved excitedly. They had never seen a plane in their lives. Then the planes flew low and began dropping bombs. Gladys and others were having their morning worship when a bomb hit the inn. Sometime later, Gladys regained consciousness and managed to crawl out from under debris. People all over the city were dead and wounded. There were no doctors. Gladys took what medicines and bandages she had and began helping. Too many had no help, and she wept with sorrow. Hundreds of people died that dreadful day.

The Japanese entered the city and then left, only to come back. Life was never the same again. Gladys still went to the villages to help as much as she could. As she traveled, she would give any military information she could discover to the struggling Chinese army. After all, these were *her* people now. Her own family grew quickly. There were so many orphans. More and more children were left at the inn or brought there by someone from the city. Gladys was their only hope.

By the spring of 1940, most of China was experiencing active warfare and the plight of the people daily grew more desperate. Each time bombers grew near, Gladys took her growing family of children to safety in nearby caves. There were soon over one hundred boys and girls at the inn. By now, Ninepence was one of the older girls.

One day, the general to whom Gladys passed information that could help the Chinese army, came to the inn to talk to her. He sounded worried. "*Ai Weh Deh* (Eye Way Duh)," he greeted her, "you must go to safety. The Japanese are soon going to take your city." Gladys looked puzzled, "But I can't leave Yangcheng and all my children!" Then she added, "Anyway, they won't hurt me, a small, unimportant woman." The general shook his head, "Oh no, my friend. You are *wanted*. There is a price on your head. You are now considered a spy!" Gladys was shocked.

If she was captured by the Japanese, what would happen to her children? And then she remembered. Word had come that Madame Chiang Kai-shek, wife of President Chiang himself, had sent a message. *Ai Weh Deh* (Eye Way Duh) could bring her children to *Xian* (She Ann) in Free China. Madame's orphanage there would keep them and feed them. Gladys knew such a trip with a hundred children, some of them toddlers, was next to impossible. But now, what *choice* did she have? None.

There was only one way out of her city to get to distant *Xian* (She Ann). It was a journey of more than four hundred miles — and the only route was over the steep mountains of *Shansi* (Shahn She) Province. Furthermore, Gladys had one hundred children dependent on *her* alone. Gladys knew she had just one source of help: Jehovah God.

The kindly Mandarin sent two of his soldiers with enough grain for several days. Then Gladys and her children were on their own. The little woman with the giant heart bravely set out, the older children helping her carry the toddlers. The task seemed impossible. In her heart, Gladys realized the gravity of her situation. She alone could not do this. Only God could. The children each had just one pair of shoes. Those soon wore out with so much walking. Each child carried a pair of chopsticks and a little tin bowl. Off they started. At first, it felt like a fun trip. Everyone joked and played as they walked and skipped along. But by nighttime, the skipping changed. It became a slow plodding, and the little ones would cry out, "Mama, I am tired. I am hungry. My feet hurt. Let's just stop."

Gladys tried everything she could to lift their spirits. They made a game of seeing how many birds they could count, or how many flowers they could find. Water was scarce and the further they went, the less food they found. A normal mother would have had to give up. Gladys Aylward was not a normal mother. She could never give up. She got the children to singing, recalling every hymn or little chorus she had ever taught them. Then they recited passages of Scripture they had learned from her.

One of their favorite songs was "Count Your Blessings." Gladys' heart failed within her as she recalled how *few* their blessings were just now. It wasn't hard for the children to fall asleep each night — even on the hard, unyielding ground. They were literally tired to the bone. Gladys herself was exhausted and aching from carrying toddlers all day. Often, she could not even sleep. Ninepence would usually snuggle up next to her adopted mother and draw strength from just resting in her presence. The darkness of the nights on a mountainside was absolute. All around them was silence. Only the occasional shuffling of a body or the sleep murmur of a little child broke the stillness.

Many a night, there popped into *Ai Weh Deh's* (Eye Way Duh's) mind a prayer that Mrs. Lawson had taught her years ago: *Dear Lord, if I must die, let me not be afraid of death, but let there be some* meaning, *O God, in my dying.* This became her prayer that entire nightmare of a journey. By God's grace, with very little food, no medical care, and little water, one hundred children and their courageous mama walked and sang and prayed for eleven endless days. They crossed countless mountain ranges. The thought ringing in Gladys' mind was, *If we can just get to the Yellow River, a ferry will take us over into Free China. Then it's on to Xian* (She Ann) *and safety.*

The morning of the twelfth day, they topped yet another mountain, and one of the boys in front yelled excitedly, "Mama San, there is the Yellow River! We made it!" Sure enough, gleaming in the sun like a wonderful ribbon of gold, lay the great Yellow River. Gladys' first thought was, *Now, to find the ferry to take us across into Free China.*

But there was no ferry. There was no boat of any kind. Now what? Gladys' weary mind could think of no answer. She felt threatened by the despair that wanted to take over her every thought. *Oh God, oh God, what can I do? They all depend on me.*

"Alright, children," Gladys spoke to her large brood, "we will wait here by the river. You can splash and wash in the water, and we will wait for a boat." The children frolicked and played as the teenagers looked after the small ones. They had never in their lives seen so much water. This was an adventure. It was more of a nightmare to Gladys.

By the morning of the third day, Gladys was close to panic. The river was swift and wide and none of these children could swim. Then *Sua Lan* (Swah Lahn), a girl of thirteen, came to Gladys, asking, "Mama

San, do you remember when you told us about Moses. You said when God called him to take the children of Israel through the Red Sea, every one of them got safely across?" "Of course I do!" Gladys replied. *Sua Lan* (Swah Lahn) smiled sweetly and asked, "Do you believe that story?" Gladys looked shocked, "Why certainly! I would not tell you a story I didn't believe!" The young girl inquired, "Then why don't *we* go across?" That shook Gladys, and she gasped, "But I'm not Moses!" *Sua Lan* (Swah Lahn) looked earnestly at her and replied, "No, but Jehovah is still God!"

Those words struck Gladys' heart like a blow. She had staked her life on God's power. He would not desert her *now*. The two of them gathered the older children around and all knelt to pray. They earnestly asked God to deliver them. Even as they were praying, one of the young boys ran up, "Mama San, there is a big man here!" Gladys rose to her feet. Seemingly out of nowhere, stood a Chinese army official. He was amazed to hear their story. The Chinese government had closed the ferry to prevent the enemy from going across. Immediately, the General gave a loud, strange whistle. In moments, an answering whistle came echoing back. Incredibly, a boat appeared, and in three trips transported all one hundred of them to the other side.

The Chinese army fed them all. Soon they were on their way to a train that could take them closer to their destination and safety. It sounded easy. But Gladys had not found anything easy in the last fifteen years. This next part of the journey was no exception. They did, however, find the train going in the direction of *Xian* (She Ann). The children were astonished — they had never seen a long black train that belched smoke. Gladys and the children traveled until the train stopped and could go no further. The enemy lay ahead. Again, they would have to walk the remaining miles. Once more, Gladys was close to collapse. *Surely, God, you didn't bring us this far just to leave us now!*

And no, He had not. The kindly station master took pity on them. There was a coal train that traveled through the night, through enemy territory. Every child must stay completely silent. The older ones cared for the little ones and cushioned them on the piles of coal headed for Xian (*She Ann*). They made it safely through the rough spots and arrived much closer to their goal the next morning. The small ones laughed in glee to see how all of them were covered with black coal dust. Gladys was just relieved to be that much closer to safety.

Again, they walked. Again, they sang. Mile after weary mile. Kind strangers along the way helped with food. After an entire month of walking, climbing, hurting, scarcely eating, and then climbing some more, the band of children and their *Ai Weh Deh* (Eye Way Duh) saw in the distance the walls of the ancient capital of China — *Xian* (She Ann). There awaited Madame Chiang's orphanage, with food and clothing and water. And safety. On the brave children and their beloved *Ai Weh Deh* (Eye Way Duh) marched, singing now with joy each step they took, "Count your blessings, name them one by one. Count your many blessings, see what God has done!" By God's grace, they were safe at last!

THE REST OF THE STORY

Miraculously, Gladys Aylward was able to reach her goal without losing one child. The many years of service that followed for her were a mixture of adventure, satisfaction, suffering, illness, persecution — and, most of all, joy. God used her in China many more years, then in England, Hong Kong, and Taiwan. She established a mission in Hong Kong and still another orphanage in Taiwan. Gladys became known around the world as the brave little woman who accomplished giant tasks for God.

The young girl who could not even complete her schooling ended up seeing that same school named "Gladys Aylward Academy." The young woman who could not pass an exam at the theological seminary learned both to speak and write the difficult Chinese language. Gladys shared the gospel with thousands and led countless people to faith in Christ. A movie was made of her life. She was honored personally by Queen Elizabeth of England. Yet she remained forever Gladys Aylward, the small woman with a giant heart.

Gladys as a young parlor maid.

Gladys, later in life, with one of her many orphans.

Gladys and her very first adopted child, Ninepence, and her daughter.

Author's Note

It was our family's privilege to know Gladys Aylward personally. She remained forever the same practical, no-nonsense little lady who loved children and served God devotedly. Gladys made no bones about being a simple person with an awesome Heavenly Father. We first knew her in Taipei, Taiwan, where she established yet another orphanage. She was welcomed royally in Taiwan and had a remarkable ministry there, both caring for children and preaching all over the island.

We were honored to frequently have Sunday lunch with her at a restaurant in Taipei. Our children were fascinated with her stories. Bob and I and our two, Alice and Jody, particularly remember having New Year's dinner with her in 1965. Alice was five at the time, and Jody, two and a half. Alice asked Miss Aylward about unbinding the feet of the little girls in the villages around Yangcheng. All of us listened intently as she told her experiences with those village children. Gladys explained, "Those little girls loved to have their aching feet unbound, washed in warm water, and rubbed until the blood would flow freely again." That New Year's Day is one our family will never forget. Gladys' little adopted boy, Gordon, was just slightly younger than Jody and they enjoyed playing together. Meeting Gladys Aylward and spending time with her was a bit like meeting history face to face.

Miss Aylward died of pneumonia in 1970, having survived countless illnesses, persecution, and near starvation. Gladys Aylward is buried in Taipei, in the Republic of China. Her memory is alive in countless countries because of her simple faith and the depth of her courage. That faith produced a harvest of souls that are now scattered across the world. Those who learned of God's love from *Ai Weh Deh* (Eye Way Duh) are still passing that love on — even unto a third and fourth generation.

Bibliography

Books and Articles

Anderson, Courtney. *To the Golden Shore.* 1st Edition. Boston: Brown and Company, 1956.

Aylward, Gladys, with Christine Hunter. *The Little Woman.* Chicago: Moody Publishers, 1970.

Burgess, Alan. *The Small Woman: The Story of Gladys Aylward.* London: Pan Books LTD, 1969.

College of Charleston (Charleston, South Carolina). Numerous articles, pictures, documents related to the Townsend family.

Durham, Jaqueline. *Miss Strong Arm: The Story of Annie Armstrong.* Nashville, Tennessee: Broadman Press, 1966.

Evans, Elizabeth Marshall. *Annie Armstrong.* Birmingham, Alabama: Woman's Missionary Union, 1963.

Hall, Gordon Langley. *Golden Boats from Burma.* Philadelphia: Macrae Smith Co., 1961.

Hunt, Rosalie Hall. *A Life Beyond Boundaries: The Extraordinary Story of Ann Hasseltine Judson.* Valley Forge, Pennsylvania: Judson Press, 2018.

-----*Bless God and Take Courage: The Judson History and Legacy.* Valley Forge, Pennsylvania: Judson Press, 2005.

-----*Guided by Grace: The Kathleen Mallory Story.* Greenville, South Carolina: Courier Publishing, 2020.

-----*Her Way: The Remarkable Story of Hephzibah Jenkins Townsend.* Greenville, South Carolina: Courier Publishing, 2016.

-----*6 Yellow Balloons: An MK's China Story.* Greenville, South Carolina: Courier Publishing, 2021.

-----*The Blue Enamel Cup: An MK's China Legacy.* Greenville, South Carolina: Courier Publishing, 2022.

Jackson, Dave and Neta. *Flight of the Fugitives.* Minneapolis, Minnesota: Bethany House Publishers, 1994.

Jennings, Jess. *Look Who God Can Use!* Orlando, Florida: 2022. Privately Published.

Judson, Edward. *The Life of Adoniram Judson.* Philadelphia: American Baptist Publication Society, 1883.

Knowles, James W. *Memoire of Mrs. Ann H. Judson, Late Missionary to Burmah,* 1st edition. Boston: Lincoln and Edwards, 1829.

McIntosh, Sherrie L. *The Old Edisto Island Baptist Church. Hephzibah Jenkins Townsend: 1780-1847 and the Inheritance of Stewardship and Spiritual Gifts.* Morgantown, West Virginia, 1998.

Sorrill, Bobbie. *Annie Armstrong, Dreamer in Action.* Nashville, Tennessee: Broadman Press, 1984.

Wyeth, Walter. *Ann H. Judson: A Memorial.* Cincinnati: Privately Published, 1888.

www.ingramcontent.com/pod-product-compliance
Lightning Source LLC
Chambersburg PA
CBHW040315170426
43196CB00020B/2927